ARTHUR DALEY'S
GUIDE TO
Doing it Right!

Leon Griffiths created the character of Arthur Daley.

ARTHUR DALEY'S GUIDE TO

Doing it Right!

Leon Griffiths

ILLUSTRATIONS BY
JOHN IRELAND

Fontana/Collins

First published by Willow Books 1985
First issued in Fontana Paperbacks 1986

Copyright © Leon Griffiths 1985

Made & printed in Great Britain by
William Collins Sons & Co. Ltd, Glasgow

For Pattie and Patsy and the old gang

Contents

ACKNOWLEDGEMENTS

The author and publishers would like to thank George Cole for all his help.

Photographic credits
TV Times/Transworld: front cover, pages 36, 53.
Thames Television: pages 1, 13, 14, 18, 33, 65, 81, 84, 88, 95, 107, 109, 110, 115.
Scope Features/John Paul: pages 85, 99.

Introduction

This modest volume is a collection of fragments, essays, anecdotes and aphorisms which may be of help to everyone who is trying to earn a crust in this highly competitive society of ours.

It is a primer for life; a ready-made philosophy for people who haven't got the time or the intelligence to suss out for themselves all the diabolical liberties inflicted on them.

I think of myself as a spokesman for the alternative economy. I don't mean the loony left or the macro-bionic minority, but people who wear suits and understand the value of a sov.

I dedicate this tome to all who have to bob and weave in life, and those who can't buy this book for half-price (they certainly need to read it).

Throughout my commercial life, I have always believed that my word is my bond. When I touch hands a deal is a deal. But may I remind you, as you venture into any enterprise or even a bit of skulduggery, you should never, never use your own money. Remember this, and as you go through life you will always be grateful that this advice was given by a true friend, yours

Arthur Daley

Early days

I had an unhappy childhood, like many other artists, writers and thrusting entrepreneurs.

So I will not dwell on the sadness. These were the hungry thirties, the lean years, when if you could nick a bottle of milk from the doorstep it could feed a family of ten for a week.

I was up for a grammar school scholarship but I did a year in an approved school instead. As usual, it was a fit-up. I was grassed. Nothing changes, eh? Judas Iscariot grassed Our Saviour. They were even at it in those days, and they didn't have a *Sunday Mirror* to sell it to. (It's become ridiculous now. I blame it on the media. You get people plotting a crime and one of them realises that the proceeds from the newspaper article would be better than the swag from the robbery. And we're not even talking about the foreign rights, TV spin-offs and the paperback.)

Many would say that I was a sensitive youth. I was good at arithmetic, history and R.E. I had more English than the teachers so I ducked that subject to pursue my extra-curricular business activities. For two years I had a monopoly of conkers in the playground, and I had a deal with a local café for surplus free school milk and the occasional jar of cod liver oil and malt. I excelled in all sports but my talent was in management rather than on the playing field. Violence was always a threat.

There were many bitter fights, particularly during boat-race week, although we had no idea where or what Cambridge and Oxford were. After all these years, I still think of myself as a Cambridge man.

My first job was as an office boy and within three weeks I had modernised the post room but the principal said, 'There's only one guv'nor in this company and it ain't you, Daley.' (He was nicked for fraud years later. So much for his business efficiency methods.)

I was trying to find a place for myself in the hurly-burly of commercial life. I tried window cleaning, a stint as a street book-maker's runner, coffee-stall assistant, barrow-boy specialising in fruit and then crockery – 'I'm offering you not one teacup and saucer, not even two, three, four or five. Here you are, lady . . . take the six of them, genuine English bone china . . . I'm losing money on them . . . I'm not even asking five shillings or four shillings or three. All I want is a half a crown. A simple tosheroon, my dear, and you can entertain the King of England for tea . . .'

This was my apprenticeship. And then the dark clouds of war rumbled.

Our finest hour

The war was the making of me like so many others: the roll-call of honour is long. Think of Montgomery, Churchill, Ernie Bevin, Glen Miller, 'Bomber' Harris (I wonder if he's the dad of 'Chopper' Harris, the Chelsea full-back?). No? Well, it was just a thought.

I loved the war. Our island race was at its best. Every man was a hero. Everybody had a job – even if they didn't want it. I liked the excitement of the blackout, mucking together in the shelters, sacrifices, the shortages, petrol coupons, clothing coupons, American soldiers with handfuls of nylon stockings – oh, happy days. If you couldn't make a crust in the war, you couldn't call yourself an Englishman.

Even the Old Bill were nicer (incidentally, we used to call them the Law in those days). And at the helm was the great man, Winston Churchill. If you want to talk about Verbal he had plenty. With modesty, I have modelled my own rhetoric style on his own.

The war years were my university. I can still remember the music of Vera Lynn, and Joe Loss was doing a gallon of brilliantine a week despite the shortages. We didn't need television, mostly because there wasn't any television. Radio was brilliant and you had to use your imagination. And it wasn't just the BBC – there was AFN, the American Forces radio, and you could hear the Inkspots from morning to night. You could dance, and I must admit that I was a fairly nifty ballroom dancer – there was the Hammersmith Palais, the Lyceum, tea dances at the old Trocadera . . . they even converted the Royal Opera House at Covent Garden into a dance hall. We were dancing towards Berlin. I often think that formation dancing is in the blood of true Englishmen.

London was the citadel of freedom. There were foreigners from all over the place – Free French, Belgians, Dutchmen, Poles, Americans, even Albanians, and they didn't understand our ways and culture or our money. I was doing my bit to help our allies. I mean, they didn't know where to find a bottle of Scotch or genuine French perfume for their girlfriends. (As I recall it, a chemist in Shepherd's Bush was knocking them out – Scotch *and* perfume.)

There was also a large regiment called the London First Trotters – men who had resigned from the hostilities, shell-shocked by the discipline of the fighting services, or the food. These people had to be sheltered, fed and clothed. They needed identity cards, ration books and petrol coupons. These unfortunate creatures couldn't be discarded by society – somebody had to look after them. Yes, it wasn't all Glen Miller and Vera Lynn, you know.

During the last months of the European war firearms appeared in London. They'd been captured from the enemy. Mausers and Walthers were part of a thriving cottage industry. As an old pal of mine said to me at the time: 'It's one of the ironies of our time. You can shoot anybody now – not just Germans.'

A SOLDIER OF THE KING

Now obviously if the war was on today I would be in the SAS. As it happens, they put me in the Royal Army Service Corps. I was ready to defend my king and country but there was nobody to fight. The Germans had quit; all they were thinking about now was conquering the world with BMWs and Volkswagens. But what was I doing? Blancoing my webbing-belt and gaiters in Catterick, square-bashing and doing my bit in the stores. Comradeship is one thing but some psychopathic sergeant telling you to polish your boots is quite another.

A couple of years in National Service would do wonders for those football hooligans and the drug fiends. I didn't need the discipline; I was already a responsible adult. Even then I was a premature Thatcherite, a self-made entrepreneur.

You have to realise when the war was over there were hundreds of 15cwt trucks and piles of heavy-duty Dunlop tyres rotting in the depot. In the world outside there were plenty of jobbing builders trying to reconstruct our blitzed cities. I felt it was my duty to help the homeless and get the economy moving. Of course, the court martial couldn't understand it. They said it was army property. Well, who owns the army? Tax-payers. I was simply liberating the assets of the population. We won a war for freedom, for the little man to get a crust, to oil the wheels of industry again. (Oh yes, there was a small question of two hundred and twenty-five gallons of oil, as well, now I remember it).

The sentence was vicious. Mind you, if Monty had known about it he would have given me a couple of stripes. He liked a bit of initiative.

Democracy means:
One man, one vote,
one Giro and one bike.

A little earner

I first saw a pound when my mother (God bless her) was searching through my dad's pockets one night. Right away I was excited. I was about two years old at the time and I liked the colour and texture of the pound note. It looked better than a golliwog and I decided to collect them. All these years later my heart still skips a beat when I see, touch or fondle a pound note. We need them. Unless you've got private means – such as an estate in Hampshire or a dad doing twenty years on the Moor but you know where the bankroll is – you'll have to have a job. Well, not a *job* – that's for workers – but an occupation or even a vocation.

Some people think of me as a general trader. I think of myself as an entrepreneur, a creative businessman.

A gentleman needs a little earner. And an 'earner' means the Nelson Eddys (readies = cash). We don't need huge stocks, capital investment, order books and the like. We're in and out merchants, 'bed and breakfast' – like the stock market gamblers.

We're looking for a modest enterprise – fruit and veg, wine bars, emergency plumbers, motorbike messenger services, sandwich bars, ticket agencies, sauna clubs, dry cleaners, driving schools or steam cleaning businesses.

You don't want staff, unless they're family (and even they can steal from you). Remember, today's employee is tomorrow's partner and partners rob you blind.

Don't trust nobody. You are the captain of your soul and (even more important) the keeper of the Jack and Jill (the till).

Here are some likely earners:

Fruit and veg If you meet a greengrocer you're meeting a rich man. Fruit-and-veg men have never heard of cheques. The whole business is run on cash. Mind you, you have to graft. Up in the morning at four o'clock, shlepping to the market, a few sacks of King Edwards, two boxes of spring onions and a bag of cauliflowers and you're in business. No VAT on the fruit and veg and you're halfway to Marbella with all the other bandits.

Even the Inland Revenue don't know how to catch your local friendly greengrocer. They're all at it – importers, wholesalers and street marketeers. 'It's the weather, guv. We've had a hot summer or a frosty winter. Half of my stock was rotten before I put it on the counter.'

Wine bars No skill required. You need a decent pitch, four pictures of St Tropez, six potted plants, a dozen empty Chianti bottles hanging from the ceiling, and the sawdust is optional. You don't have to know about wine – what is there to know? All you have to do is draw a cork and count the money. The mark-up is at least 300 per cent and often more.

Emergency plumbers Before you call an emergency plumber, why don't you phone a Harley Street brain surgeon? He'd probably do it better and cheaper too. Once an emergency plumber has set foot in your abode you're flushing money down the drain.

The beauty of starting an emergency plumbing service is that you don't have to know anything about cisterns, ballcocks, S-bends or washers. All you need is a couple of telephones and the numbers of local plumbers. You cop on commission.

Messenger services First you need a dozen eager young lads on the rock-and-roll (dole) with their own motor cycles. You advertise in the local newspaper or *The Standard* and wait for the first customer. An office, shed or even a coal-hole is handy for the phone. Speed is the curse of our society. That's why

every third vehicle on the roads is delivering a message –
from publishers to printers, architects to building sites,
advertising agencies to clients, chemists to doctors or
wholesalers to retailers. Whatever happened to postmen?

Sandwich bars Most sandwich-bar owners can do with one
tomato as our Lord Jesus Christ did with a handful of fish and
rolls. He knew what he was doing. If you can run a wine bar
you can run a sandwich bar – and you don't need the empty
Chianti bottles hanging from the ceiling. Mother's Pride is
your greatest friend, with margarine (healthy as well) and
plenty of Provencal pâté and lettuce. When I was a lad, pâté
was called fish paste or meat paste and they still taste just the
same. Instant coffee in plastic cups is more expensive than
Tattinger to the punter.

There are always opportunities for those who duck and dive or bob and weave. The video game was one for those who got up early in the morning and there are other early mornings ahead – computer games, charities, driving schools, short-lease flats and time-share castles in Spain, Scotland, Wales, Switzerland or Florida. (You'll say there are *no* castles in Florida. But I can tell you that there will be.)

Ticket agencies You don't need an office so you operate from home. You're not really a ticket agency – you're more a broker. Some people say that you're a tout. Who cares, eh? First you supply for all the big sporting fixtures, concerts, shows and events.

Sometimes you have to queue up like ordinary people, or you get ten other people to queue up for you. You pick carefully. The Cup Final is a banker, no matter who's playing. But you don't want to know about England *v* Cyprus or even England *v* East Germany. Wimbledon is a cert. You can advertise tickets for that in *The Times*. Ditto the Royal Ballet, Ol' Blue Eyes' eighty-first farewell concert at the Royal Albert Hall, the return of The Who, the return of the Rolling Stones, the return of Edward Heath, the return of Henry Cooper plays Rodgers and Hart. The return of somebody is always a winner. We're a very sentimental race.

Mind you, there are a few wicked people in the game. A pal of mine bought 200 tickets for the single-handed-sailing-boat-round-the-world-race. Obviously you have to think first . . . know what I mean?

Rules for the budding entrepreneur:
- DEMAND CASH FROM THEM, BUT ALWAYS GIVE THEM A CHEQUE.

- SELL BEFORE YOU BUY.

You've got to get on your toes. There is always a market and a price. Be busy. No matter what they want you can get it for them . . . a second-hand video machine or jumbo jet. But always get a deposit. You may never see him again — and vice versa.

Throughout my business career I have said: 'My word is my bond — usually'. But occasionally the fertile ground is parched. It happens to the best of us whether he be Sir Freddie Laker, Onassis or me. Cash flow stutters. It may be industrial unrest, the commodities market, the dollar being sluggish, the oil crisis, or the grain harvest in the Ukraine. But, on my landlord's life, I haven't got the dough. There is then the problem of an early holiday or soldiering on. What about the unpaid bill? The classic riposte is, 'The cheque is in the post.' Or you can send a cheque but don't sign it. That way you get three days' leeway and if you can't get money in three days then you shouldn't be in business anyway.

Others suggest that you go to your solicitor and question the creditor's demand. Or offer them a token – three reconditioned sewing machines, four North Korean transistor radios and a dozen bottles of Albanian sparkling wine. Barter is coming back, particularly in the alternative economy.

Even a Crown Court will give you time to pay. And if there's a threat of physical violence you have to call on your minder. That's his job. Make sure you always pay his wages regularly and a couple of Bonios as well.

BUILDING CONVERSIONS

Rome wasn't built in a day but at least they knew what they were doing.

If you can fill a shelf in Tesco's you're on the way to being able to convert a Victorian house. The new generation of builders think that City and Guilds is a new pub selling real ale.

Do you ever have the feeling that there are now more builders than buildings? But they're all working, except on Tuesday mornings because that's when they sign on. The average builder's estimate is trying for the Booker Prize. Four months later when you question the new kitchen units, he'll say: 'I didn't know you wanted water as well. We'll have to plumb it out from the mains. It's gonna cost you . . .'

Most jobs consist of knocking down walls and then making-do with filler. They're astonished to be asked to build a wall, like with bricks and cement and all those traditional skills. 'Why don't you have a hardboard panel instead with a simulated stripped pine veneer on the top?' they'll suggest. If they don't know how to do it – and they usually don't – they're off to the local Do-It-Yourself shop to ask the bloke behind the counter.

How to run a successful business empire

For all you budding entrepreneurs, here is an example of a successful business empire – Daley Enterprises (International) Ltd. You may find that it acts as an inspiration to you when you are starting out in your own first business enterprise.

Structure of Daley Enterprises (International) Ltd.

Daley Enterprises (International)

Leisure Activities

Marbella Sauna Club

A.D.Video Services

Anglo-American Computer Games

Las Vegas Machines Inc.
one-armed bandits

Ace Aquariums
Everything for tropical fish

Old Masters
picture framing service
Manager: D.Hockney

Tickets Galore
From Wembley to Wimbledon ticket agency

A.D.Personal Security
Principal: T.McCann

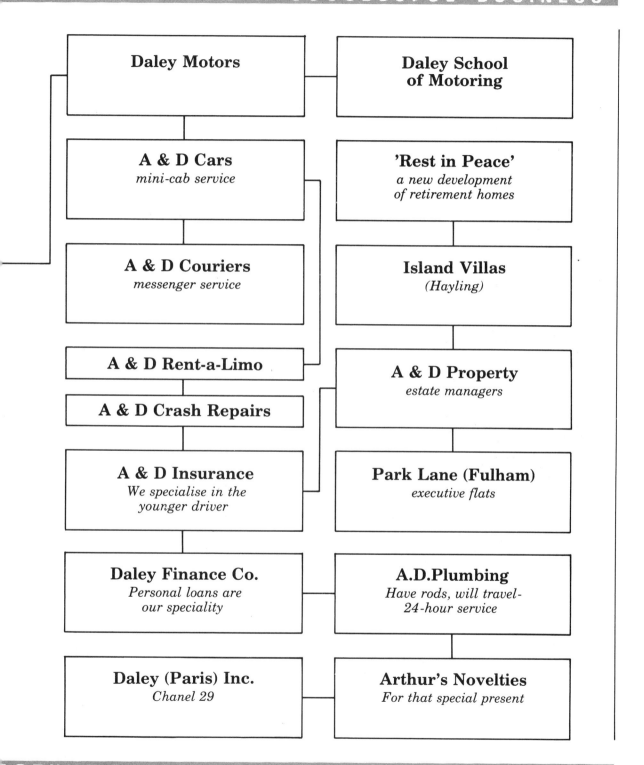

Daley Motors

Daley School
of Motoring

A & D Cars
mini-cab service

'Rest in Peace'
*a new development
of retirement homes*

A & D Couriers
messenger service

Island Villas
(Hayling)

A & D Rent-a-Limo

A & D Property
estate managers

A & D Crash Repairs

A & D Insurance
*We specialise in the
younger driver*

Park Lane (Fulham)
executive flats

Daley Finance Co.
*Personal loans are
our speciality*

A.D.Plumbing
*Have rods, will travel-
24-hour service*

Daley (Paris) Inc.
Chanel 29

Arthur's Novelties
For that special present

You and your accountant

The relationship between you and your accountant is a special and sensitive one. He knows everything about you and you know nothing about him. You trust him and he doesn't believe a word you say. You admit your sins and he's going to give you the nod of approval if not absolution.

For the privilege of hearing your innermost secrets he wants money as well.

The best accountant is one who is creative and wants to beat the system but he hasn't the bottle to do it himself. He needs a client like me. Let him teach you. But don't let him dominate you. They still believe that two plus two makes four. But because you are an instinctive entrepreneur you know that two plus two makes whatever you want.

The name of the game is to present financial statements without incurring tax liability. I have done this throughout my life and if the accountant doesn't like it he can always go elsewhere.

My current accountant is a willing chap and he likes a drink, but there have been delays in finalising the accounts. He is a pessimist while I am an optimist. He values the 'lease and goodwill' at £23,500.50; my own valuation is much higher. I know the place, don't I? And at £424,100.00 it's a steal, or at least a bargain. (With those figures I may even be able to get a bank loan.) Remember, accountants are not businessmen. And my own accountant realises that occasionally I have a cash flow problem. Because of that he took a six-year-old Lancia (a nice little runner, though) in lieu of his fees last year.

DALEY ENTERPRISES (INTERNATIONAL) LTD – DIRECTOR'S REPORT

The Director submits his report and the audited accounts for the year ended 31 December, 1979.

BUSINESS REVIEW

The company is a conglomerate and carries out the following activities:

Motor sales	– the purchase and sale of exclusive motors
Motor repairs	– satisfaction guaranteed
School of motoring	– first-time passes a speciality
Insurance	– policies for the younger driver personally guaranteed. 'Our premiums are never beaten'
Personal security	– Mr Arthur Daley provides his personal services together with those of his chief assistant Mr Terence McCann
Leisure activities	– provision of amusement machines on premises frequented by the public
Retail/wholesale buying and selling	– anything considered
Plumbing emergency services	– a man will be on your doorstep within the hour
Old Master framing	– security guaranteed
Property services	– estates management

Associated company:

Messenger services	– we get there first

DIRECTOR

The sole director is Mr Arthur Daley who is the holder of 100 per cent of the company's share capital.

AUDITORS

Messrs Milligan, Watershed & Co. resigned on 1 April, 1984. Messrs Tremble & Potts were appointed on 2 April, 1984 and resigned on 9 April, 1984. Messrs Grabble & Co. were appointed auditors on 10 April, 1984. A resolution to re-appoint them as auditors will be proposed at the Annual General Meeting.

BY ORDER OF THE BOARD

Date: 31 December 1979
Registered office: Liechtenstein

BALANCE SHEET
as at
31 December, 1979

	£	£
Lease and Goodwill		424,100
Fixtures, fittings	4,000	
Less: aggregate depreciation	400	
		3,600
Current assets:		
Stock in hand	116,320	
Sundry debtors	9,296	
		125,616
		553,316
Less sundry creditors:		
Sundry creditors	189,416	
Bank overdraft	36,104	
		225,520
		327,796
Represented by:		
Share capital:		
Authorised 100 shares of £1 each		100
Issued: fully paid 2 shares of £1 each		2
Capital reserve (see Note 4)		407,929
Profit and loss account – deficit		(80,133)
		327,796

TRADING AND PROFIT AND LOSS ACCOUNT
for the year ended
31 December, 1979

	£	£
SALES		137,101
Deduct: Stock at 1 January, 1984	79,942	
Purchases	136,619	
	216,561	

	£	£
Less:		
Stock at 31 December, 1979	116,320	
(see *Note 1*)		100,241
GROSS PROFIT		36,860
Receipts for services and rents		41,222
		78,082
Less: Expenditure		
Rent and rates	15,420	
Telephone	1,992	
Light and heat	774	
Freelance salaries (inc. bodyguards)	37,319	
Travelling	18,932	
Entertaining foreign visitors	11,041	
Use of Winchester for business meetings	3,694	
Legal fees (see *Note 2*)	5,631	
Tips	3,193	
Sundry expenses	4,157	
Audit fees	1,040	
Director's remuneration – A. Daley	3,000	
Depreciation	100	
(see *Note 3*)		106,293
LOSS FOR THE YEAR		28,211
ADD: Losses brought forward from previous years		51,922
DEFICIT carried forward		80,133

NOTES TO ACCOUNTS
For the year ended
31 December, 1979

NOTE 1 STOCK
        As valued by the Managing Director

NOTE 2 LEGAL FEES
        Relate to the defence against spurious legal claims
        by customers

NOTE 3 DEPRECIATION
        Depreciation is calculated at 2½ per cent per annum,
        on a straight line basis

NOTE 4 LEASE AND GOODWILL
        Valued by the Managing Director Mr Arthur Daley

This septic island

I am a militant capitalist, true-blue, C of E, an Englishman to the core. But I ask you, is the economy healthy? Not for a moment would I question Maggie's policies. It's not her fault that three and a half million are on the cobbles. Most of them are skiving or malingering; half of the time they're tucked up in their kip reading the *Mirror* and drinking cups of tea. They don't even get up to look at TV-am.

But I remember the old days when this was the workshop of the world. We used to make things – railway engines, universal grinding machines, reels of cotton, knives and forks, shirts, ships and even shoes. Nowadays we entrepreneurs are selling things to each other and most of them are made in Japan. And what about South Korea? A trail-breaker in the new technology. I mean, they only heard about the wheel fifty years ago and now they're making motors. And we're buying them as well.

Sad, innit. Sometimes I think of this country as a double-glazed Disneyland, set in the middle of the North Sea full of oil the British can't even buy, inhabited by pop singers with orange hair selling antique pine furniture, making Burberry coats and sturdy brogues, supping soup from Wedgwood bowls or Toby jugs, scooting down with a Sinclair runabout to respray the old vintage Rolls Royce. As I said, it's not Maggie's fault, but is this England?

A rollcall of history

Every young person should study history.
The rich pageantry of the past is the heritage of
us all.

1066 The Normans landed at Hastings; and it's the only thing
that's happened there since, except for the odd county
cricket match. The Normans were the first Common
Marketeers.

1918 The end of the Great War.

1926 General Strike. Arthur Scargill's granddad was behind that.

1931 Fulham beat Torquay 10–2 and won the Third Division
championship.

1939 The start of the Second World War. Petrol rationing started
on 23 September.

1941 Clothing coupons appeared on 1 June.

1944 D-Day – that was a return match for the Normans.

1945 7 May, VE Day.

1947 The jewels in our crown, India and Pakistan, became
independent countries. Just think what we gave them –
railways, cricket, take-away curries and education, and all
that so two million of 'em could become newsagents and
tobacconists.

1948 The first Pakistani corner-shop opened in Britain.

1949 15 March – the end of clothing coupons and the end of a nice
little earner for some.

1950 26 May – the end of petrol coupons. I know a bloke who's
still got 4,000 books of them.

1960 MoT certificates were introduced.

1962 Cortinas appeared – a new dimension in get-away cars –
anonymous, dependable, a bit of poke and easy to steal.

1963 The first English villain discovered Marbella; it was like
Columbus finding the New World. Within two years you
could get Bacardi and coke, Directors' bitter, and roast beef,
Yorkshire pudding and two veg just like your mum used to
cook. Top brass from the Old Bill got so nostalgic that they

all went there for their holidays just to meet the chaps they used to interview every two weeks.

Henry Cooper knocked down Cassius Clay (a.k.a Muhammad Ali) and then invented Brut.

1966 Just in time for the World Cup, Barclaycards first appeared. Members of the alternative economy couldn't believe their luck. Not only could you go into a shop and buy things with a little piece of plastic, but they were handy for opening Yale locks as well.

Enter the gladiators, eleven English heroes, men of the bulldog breed, worthy to grace an English Parthenon, shoulder-to-shoulder with the likes of Nelson, Kitchener, Florence Nightingale, Mary Quant, Andrew Fleming and Ivor Novello.

That afternoon, 30 July, the streets were empty. Even the tea-leaves stayed at home. There was a lump in the throat when the great Bobby Moore brandished the Cup to the crowd. The Germans had a few lumps as well, all over the place, after Nobby Stiles got into them. The score was England 4–West Germany 2, though how they ever did it with Labour in control, I really don't know.

1968 The Post Office introduced Giro, a new way of paying your bills. This became so popular with the Government that it was soon sending cheques to three and a half million people, a perfect vindication of a system that nobody could understand.

The breathalyser was first used. This was to stop people spending their Giro payments on alcohol or new Mercedes', which were now fashionable with football club chairmen.

1970 A sad day for England. Bobby Moore, captain of England, got nicked in Bogota, Columbia, on his way to Mexico for the World Cup. There's Bobby, clean-limbed, a perfect specimen of English manhood, never been in bother, no previous, never known to mix with bad company, and he gets his collar felt. It just shows you – Old Bill is Old Bill, no matter where you are. Thank gawd he had a good brief.

1971 The year of decimalisation. Old ladies couldn't understand it but every shopkeeper got the idea within a minute; mark up rather than mark down. In a month there were thousands of millionaires in halfpennies.

1972 The first big batch of Japanese motors hit the roads. The video revolution. Philips marketed the first domestic video recorder followed by the Japanese. It took a few years before the great public got the idea and by that time there were more pirates down every High Street than on the Spanish Main.

1973 VAT – the most iniquitous, diabolical tax ever invented, and it was old Teddy Heath who was at the helm that time. Mind you, there's always a silver lining – if you're an astute general dealer you can always put the VAT on an item but you don't have to send it to HM Customs and Excise, do you? However, it is advisable to change your address every two years. Those computers aren't all that clever, are they?

1975 What with India, the MoT and VAT we done another ricket – the Common Market. All I ask is how many Maestros have we sold in Europe? We're all eating croissants with our coffee, crunching French apples and drinking Belgian lager but what's in it for us?

1979 Maggie does it – she becomes Prime Minister. Let the people free, she said, and right away prices went up, unemployment went up, inflation went up, police pay went up . . . how did she get in, I wonder?

1982 The jewel in Maggie's crown. The British lion swished its tail and defeated Argentina. It was almost as good as the World Cup. Our lads liberated 600,000 sheep and 1,800 people who wanted a free health service and all the other benefits of our society. The Arthur Daley Travel Service was one of the first companies offering 12 nights in Port Stanley and a night in the Azores, full board and a balcony is a supplement. But business is sluggish.

1984 The enemy within raised its head. It cost a few bob but at least we saw out Arthur Scargill and his mutinous crew. However, I'm as loyal as the next man and I'm not knocking Maggie or Peter Walker, Man of the Match, but I've got 800 bags of Coalite and a dozen gross of candles in the lock-up and what am I going to do with them?

18 August. There it was in two-inch letters right across the front page of the *Sun*: ' 'ER INDOORS IS MUGGED!' Even I was surprised, but it shows the kind of muscle I've got.

What is a 'drink'?

If you don't know what a 'drink' is then I'm talking to a man from outer space.

A 'drink' is universal currency. Politicians take a drink, ministers take a drink, judges, lawyers, policemen, councillors, aldermen, footballers, managers, boxers, coppers, taxi drivers, builders . . . they all understand the meaning of a drink.

A drink can be (a) a pleasantry, (b) a favour, (c) a piece of the action, (d) a present, (e) a simple tip, (f) a bribe.

There are different kinds of drinks.

1 There's a *drink* in it for you, old son.
2 There's a *little drink*, etc.
3 There's a **nice** *little drink*, etc.
4 There's a **good** *little drink*, etc.
5 There's a *large drink*, etc.
6 There's a *handsome* drink, etc.

We live in cynical times. The man with his hand out is offering a service and you reject him at your peril. That doesn't mean you have to spoil him.

Take, for example, if a delivery man brings a chair and you tell him that 'there's a drink in it for you' if he takes it to the fifth floor – then you give him a *real* drink. Say to him: 'What would you fancy – a small sherry or a large Ribena?' And make sure he doesn't nick anything when he goes down.

All classes of tradesmen and repair men are prone to the 'there's a drink in it for you' strategy – particularly representatives of the major companies and the state industries. They're always ready for a bit of bunce or bungaroo. The gas man tells you that your boiler is on the blink and he has to go back to the depot for spares and it's got to be at least a week because his mate has to go to hospital and anyway there's an overtime ban and the estimate will be an arm and a leg and that particular boiler is obsolete, in my considered opinion, and it wasn't all that much cop originally anyway.

You give him a bit of that – pondering, chewing your lip, screwing up your eyes – and suggest why don't you come back in your own time without all the aggravation of crippled mates, mislaid spares, overtime bans and ten-mile hikes to the depot? Why don't you do it in your leisure? And, obviously, there's a nice little drink in it for you, old son. This same gas man, once stroppy, awkward and bolshie, is now fawning all over the gaff. And he, personally, will collect the spares in his Aston Martin Volante. (Greed is a wonderful thing.)

This routine can also be utilised on Hoover men, electricians, TV men, plumbers, carpet cleaners, glaziers, or even a tree surgeon if you've got floodlight.

And talking about surgeons, have I told you about 'er indoors' operation? She had one of those female complaints and an operation was advised. Obviously, I went to the top man and I pleaded poverty in a dignified way – like the upper classes, explaining the recession, school fees, no more winter sports and you can't get staff any more despite the unemployed ligging around the streets. I was hoping for a discount for cash. And this distinguished consultant surgeon with his piercing blue eyes, like they have, told me that he was doing a certain number of similar operations on the National Health. Was he giving me the nod? I mean, it's the same operation. He uses the same scalpels, instruments, cotton and needle – he wasn't creeping off to Corrigans to get the knife, was he? The same operation and 'er indoors and the captain's lady and Mrs O'Grady have got the same organs, haven't they?

So, I put her on the list. The surgeon had done me a favour. And just to make sure that 'er indoors was right on the top of the list I gave this famous consultant surgeon a handsome drink.

I told this account to Dave, who is a friend and a confidant, but occasionally a bit naïve, and he was astonished.

'You can't do that,' he said. 'What next . . . the parish priest, the chairman of the British Legion, lady magistrates? You can't give a drink to a surgeon.'

All I could say to Dave was simple enough. 'He bloody took it.'

If you don't pay your wages,
at least give him a drink.

The game of life

Since Socrates up to Bertrand Russell and Brian Clough thinkers have tried to solve the riddle of life. Life is just a game. And as in most games there is a scoring system. In football it's called goals, in rugby tries, cricket runs, bridge points. In life there is also a scoring system. It's called money. Whoever amasses the most pounds, dollars, roubles, rupees or yen is adjudged the winner. It's simple, innit?

THE SIMPLE FACTS OF LIFE

I see mugs all around me. I see opportunities, possibilities, expectations and bargains and deals. I'm an honest trader.

When I do business I give them my hand and my heart. Obviously, they'd rather have a receipt and a guarantee, but you can't have everything, can you?

If you want after-sales service and a warranty, go to Harrods. But if you want a quick deal for readies, I'm your man. I think of myself as the people's commercial champion, a buccaneer of the alternative economy. I don't take credit cards or cheques so don't ask.

The commercial world is based on trust. You pay your debts. It's a simple system. If you eat the lunch, pay the bill. If you want to hear the music, pay the band. Nothing's for free, that's for sure; and if it is they'll bung VAT on it. There's no way out.

I have to emphasise this cardinal rule. If you work for a guv'nor you expect to have your wages on Friday. This is the trust between the employer and his employee. Without trust the system doesn't work.

Now, unfortunately, there are a few transgressors – the slippery ones and the downright dishonest ones. Because of these scallywags we have to have laws. And to enforce these laws we have – your friend and mine – Old Bill.

Some people say that I employ a minder. What a ridiculous word with all its connotations of protector and hired muscle! My good friend Terry McCann is an employee, an invoice chaser, a *reminder* that certain people have certain responsibilities.

The early bird gets nicked by the VAT man. Never appear at your place of business before noon. Inspectors from the Inland Revenue or Customs and Excise like to keep their afternoons free for paperwork.

Advice to a young man

Many people think that I exploit my good friend and colleague, Terry McCann. This is not true. I am a fair and generous employer. But I worry about him. I've told him many times that the world is a market and we all have our little stall. The man who shouts loudest is the one that gets listened to. But what about Terence? He ain't selling anything. I see him now – a failure on the scrapheap of life, not a stamp on his card and his future behind him. To be a bird-bandit is not enough.

He's a good lad, though. A staunch friend – loyal, willing, courageous, double-honest and steadfast. He has all the good qual-

ities that we value; in fact, he's a human labrador. I'm sure he'd bring my slippers if I asked him.

We have to remember about his unfortunate history and his close encounter with the law. Not many employers would have given him a second chance. Of course, he wanted to have a regular job; a wet-nurse who would take care of his problems, pay his insurance stamps, settle his PAYE, give him holiday money and organise his pension fund. Instead, I made him stand on his own feet. I told him I was offering him the chance to be a freelance person, self-employed, his own guv'nor, which is the ambition of every true red-blooded Englishman.

Alas, he's a fool to himself. After several years I have to confess that, although young Terence is a natural worker, *he is not executive material, not in a million years. He's never going to get the board-room toilet key.*

He thinks of himself as a free spirit. But I've told him, 'We all have to compromise. You must trim sails, cut corners, bite your tongue, clench your fists, look before you leap, fib a bit, and don't be so bloody honest.'

Everybody is given a chance but if you don't take it you're going to be like all the other civilians. Think of 'er indoors' brother. He was very good at biology at school, but he frittered away his time going to youth clubs, coffee bars and reserve matches at Fulham. He could have been a doctor – now he's a consultant porter at New Charing Cross Hospital. 'At least I'm in the medical game,' he says. But it's a long way from Harley Street, innit?

Motors

The motor is the man. Tell me his motor and I'll tell you his past, his present and his aspirations. Years ago you could tell a man by his clothes. No longer. Now they're dashing around in boiler suits, cotton pickers' dungarees and unemployed joggers' gear. Yesterday's battledress is today's blouson. Whatever happened to the English gentleman's suit? I'll tell you what – only me and Prince Charles and Michael Heseltine wear three-piece suits these days. So you can't suss out a man by his shmutter any more, but you can by his motor. What about those *Saab 900 Turbo* drivers? They're most likely architects living in Islington with a cottage in Norfolk, graphic designers (whatever they are) or BBC TV cameramen.

Japanese sports car: you might find a hairdresser (who knows a couple of pop group singers) driving one because he can't afford a Porsche.

Renault 5: lady social workers, teachers and young wives dropping the kids off at the nursery.

Range Rover: they'd love to be country gentlemen but most of them are antique dealers.

Ford Escort XR3: striving salesmen shooting up the motorway with an order book.

Mercedes: they really are country gentlemen. A couple of Purdies in the back with fishing tackle and a brace of smoked salmon.

BMW: they're ambitious people. From the cheapest model to the very expensive one you'll find reliable drivers behind the steering wheel. Cautious punters who understand the value of a pound. Patriotic to the man but they'll have a foreign car.

Most punters are turned over the minute they go into a motor showroom. But perhaps I can help them. You may even get ahead of the game. There are some special rules, like:

Remember, a motor dealer is a greedy man – and I should know. If there's a sniff of real money in the air he'll spear the punter on the floor rather than have him get away. How can you suggest to him that you're a real, genuine, 18-carat punter? By showing your *wedge* – a wedge being a bundle of banknotes, the higher the denomination the better. Two hundred £20-notes would make him swoon, his mouth would froth and his brow would sweat. Well, maybe not – but he might offer you a cup of tea.

You are in control. You're holding, as we say, and he's not. Previously, a friend of yours has had a look at the motor, clocking the speedo, the music, the wheels and the extras. Now you inspect the engine and click your teeth and mutter under your breath, as if you know about mechanical things. You're on a good wicket – the average dealer wouldn't know the difference between a McPherson strut and a convertible ashtray. Make him sweat. Have a drive in the car and tell the dealer that you really like the motor, and in fact you've seen it in the window for at least three weeks. Mind you, it's a bit pricier than you wanted. The greedy dealer is wondering how big your wedge is, and he hasn't had a tickle for three days.

Let us imagine that the price is £5,000. The dealer bought the car at, say, £3,500 or less at an auction or in part exchange. He's looking for a 40–45 per cent profit in cold blood. You'll offer him £3,500 and he'll say: 'You're talking about silly money.' They always say that. *I* say it and he'll say it. 'Silly money' – it's a reflex action to a derisory offer. But he hasn't kicked you out of the place.

We are now playing poker but you've got an ace in the hole – the wedge. Yes, you're going to haggle but eventually you have to present your wedge.

'Look,' you say, 'I've got four grand, not a penny less, not a penny more. I want the motor and I've got the dough. Fair's fair . . . I saw another model down the road but I fancy yours. It's up to . . .'

At that moment, you do something dramatic like flicking the folding notes or even walking towards the door. It's you or him, no turning back. And then he'll crack. The thought of four grand walking down the street when it could be in his pocket is beyond his belief. As I said, a motor dealer is a greedy man.

If you've got the flavour of selling or buying motors I append some favourite gambits:

Ford
buying The people's car – just as Tesco is the people's shop. Have you got my drift? You don't see the Queen or Joan Collins in an Escort.
selling All over the world you'll find a Ford. Spares, no problems; service, brilliant.

Porsche
buying They just fall out of bed, pricewise.
selling Genius on four wheels.

All Italian cars
buying Little legs, Italians. Even the cigar lighter has got rust.
selling Look at their history, art and culture. Leonardo whatsisname and all the others. They more or less invented the racing car.

Jaguar

buying Yeah, it's all right if you've got four dozen dresses on the back seat. Do you really want to look like a bookmaker/villain/dress shop owner/property developer, etc?

selling The best car in the world. I personally drive one myself. Can I say more?

Volvo

buying The thing about Swedes is that they're always committing suicide. I ask myself is it because of their boring motors?

selling Do you love your kids? Do you value family life, even your grandmother? Safety is the name of the game in Sweden.

Lada

buying Do you want a Communist car, made by slave labour? It drives like a tank and is probably designed like one.

selling I'm as anti-Communist as the next man . . . but you have to think about their space programme. It ain't all ballet and combine harvesters. No strikes over there: they control things better, including quality. I know it's not pretty but it's built to last – what with their winters and everything . . . I call it a traditional motor.*

Rover

buying Old fashioned. I don't want to knock British workmanship, but . . .

selling The old values, eh? British workmanship at its best. If it's good enough for the Old Bill then it's good enough for me.

Reliant Scimitar

buying Princess Anne has got one, know what I mean?

selling Princess Anne has got one, know what I mean?

---

* *Editor's note:* Mr Daley bought three models recently and is having a hard time selling them.

Under the floorboards

At last you've got some dough but now the question is, how are you going to keep it? There is a conspiracy in the country to stop decent people having a few bob in their piggy-banks.

As the philosopher said, 'You can't take it with you' but why give it to the tax-man? I mean, he's got his pension. Some people suggest that you should invest in a building society, shares or even a deposit account at your bank. They are always going on about working hard, getting on your bike or even getting in your Jaguar 3.4, saving money for a rainy day, a hedge for inflation – but the tax-man won't let you. Once you get into the system they're after you; just a sniff of moody money and they'll capture you.

Who can you trust? In my long experience the answer is nobody. Your floorboards are as good as anything; safe deposit vaults are as vulnerable as the man who made them. There are still quite a few long-standing members of the alternative economy around who remember with horror the robbery at Lloyds Bank safe deposit vaults in Baker Street. At least in your own home you've got a piece of Wilton on the floorboards and you can sit up all night with a shotgun on your knees if you so desire.

Gold is the universal currency. Jewellery brings less than you think when you try to sell it. A plastic bag full of krugerrands or mapleleafs (Canadian) minted in pure gold is your best hedge against inflation. All you've got to worry about now is carpet cleaners, builders, plumbers and decorators . . . and the mice.

A touch of class

I mix with all classes. Dukes and dustmen, I am at ease with them all (particularly dustmen because they occasionally get a tickle and they know where to come). Things have changed in this country. We used to know where we were. I put it down to the swinging sixties. You can't have cockney models, cockney photographers and people on the BBC with Northern accents. We may have won the World Cup but we lost the old traditional values. Even Harold Wilson didn't look like a Socialist. People got too lippy and the trade unions thought they were running the country.

I see it now – all self, self, self. You give 'em a music centre and then they want a video; six months later they want a portable TV for the bedroom. You give the wife a food mixer and suddenly the kids want electric toothbrushes. I admit it's good for me, but is it good for England?

In the old days, would you imagine asking Dickie Valentine about his views on life, philosophy, Polaris and the Western alliance? But these so-called pop stars can have a chat with the Archbishop of Canterbury, Cabinet Ministers and Claire Rayner; any minute one of them is going to be elevated to the House of Lords. All these Trotskyites, lesbians, militant tendencies, one-parent families for peace, allotment holders against the bomb and the like are for a classless society. What silly people. What would happen to football without demarcations? You have to strive from the Fourth Division to the First.

I think of myself as upwardly mobile. Yes, I used to be working class – but we've all got to start somewhere, haven't we? I would never presume to be upper class or aristocracy but I'm on the way. I would describe myself as upper middle class verging towards the lower reaches of the élite class. I am certainly *not* ordinary middle class. By that I mean I have real antique furniture in my family apartment (not a flat or maisonette, you see) and I have three Victorian watercolours, a repro. Adam fireplace and I've never used hire purchase. Two kids at a private school and an executive motor and I haven't paid income tax for seven years. What else d'you want?

THE CLASS SYSTEM

My own credit-rating system is:

Working class They live in council flats with a laminated sideboard, patterned wallpaper, a video and they depend on the DHSS. They have their dinner at half past twelve and at six o'clock they have their tea (the main meal) and a snack or supper at half past nine. Lots of bread, tinned fruit, ham and stews.

Upper working class They've got a video and record player and the same dinner-tea pattern. Member of the Loan Club and saving up the deposit for a house. They love take-away Chinese meals.

Lower middle class A mortgage and a bank account and a teak veneer sideboard. They have an automatic toaster and lunch at lunchtime, tea at teatime and dinner at seven o'clock. Keen on chops and puddings with cream.

Middle class Mortgage, obviously. Joint bank account, lunch and dinner and they know who Delia Smith is. They're heavily into casseroles and spaghetti. Video, hi-fi, two transistor radios. Thinking about joining a private medical insurance organisation.

Upper middle class Period house or flat. Antique sideboard. Two bank accounts. Lunch at lunchtime. Dinner at eight. Old video, custom hi-fi. Private medical insurance. Steak, fish. Two cars, one of them being a BMW. A place in the country.

Upper class Georgian house. They never talk about money. Several bank accounts. No video, account at Harrods. Lunch at lunchtime. Dinner at 8.30. Roasts and game, simple puddings. Small estate.

Flash rich They look at *Dallas* and they'd like to be in it. They've got a swimming pool, a Roller, *three* videos, a camera and a motor cruiser. They've got at least two hundred grand in readies in a plastic bag buried in the back garden and they usually live in Essex.

Cultured class They have lots of lunches and are always pleading poverty. They work in the media or in advertising and they know about video. They're into fashion and up-to-date slang. They're all over the place.

How to spot a gentleman

Well, for a start you're not going to see them on public transport. If they live in London they use black cabs, not mini-cabs. They dress conservative and vote Tory. You'll never see gentlemen wearing T-shirts, jeans or plimsolls unless they're on a yacht.

They read the *Daily Telegraph* and they have highly-polished shoes or brogues.

They don't shout at people, even if they've got the hump. Their style is a quiet rebuke instead of a bawling-out. That's why you never hear them swear. They're punctual, modest, honest and loyal; they remember their friends – the ones they met at the old school. Look at their memoirs – they're always reminiscing about school chums who became generals, chairmen of merchant banks, presidents of the Royal Academy, cabinet ministers and members of the Jockey Club. Well, you don't get that from the local comp, do you?

I admire their accents. They get that from Uxbridge (although I'm surprised they have a university in a place like that). And what about their breakfasts? They're well into devilled kidneys, scrambled eggs and kippers and a quick stroll round the old estate. You're not going to find them living in Wigan, Bolton, Clydebank or even Milton Keynes.

Most gentlemen wear a hat. They don't pry into your affairs. I mean, if you meet one at a reception or party he's not going to give you a tug and ask: 'I say, what do you do, old chap?' Of course he won't. That's very gauche; it's the sort of remark they say in Hampstead or Primrose Hill.

Should you meet a gentleman and ask him what *he* does you're going to get a frosty answer like, 'What's it to do with you, sunshine?' That's what we call a quiet rebuke.

Gentlemen always respect their betters just as they expect to be respected by their inferiors and peers.

There's another thing about gentlemen – they always rinse their dentures before they go to bed.

A gentleman's wardrobe

Well, you don't have to go to Savile Row. Of course, it's nice – three fittings, a scone with your tea, ten weeks' wait, three parking tickets and £750 to £950 per lump. George the Greek, with his loyal staff of Asian tailors, does the same suit for £400 and you don't need an appointment. Yeah, the same suit made by one of those fine old English names like Pillock, Kilroy and Brainstorm. He'll even give you the label as well.

What you want is a handsome eighteen-ounce piece of worsted, three button, button one, four buttons on the cuff and a buttonhole on the sober lapel. We're not in the business of fashion – that's for pop stars, advertising executives and footballers. Your basic fitted wardrobe is:

Doing it right
Four suits, two sports jackets, two pairs of cavalry twill strides, ten shirts (a clean shirt every day), one velvet smoking jacket, two pairs of Oxford shoes and two pairs of brogues, heavy dark Crombie overcoat plus a camel-hair coat and a mac (Burberry), two trilbies and a tweed hat (we're not competing with Malcolm Allison or Elton John), a shooting jacket and a decent umbrella.

Doing it wrong
Windcheaters, T-shirts, blousons, silly shirts with no collars, knitted ties, leather jackets, trainers, loafers, sandals, cowboy boots and any footwear with straps, buttons or zips, patterned sweaters, donkey jackets, corduroy (which makes people look like artists, poets or documentary film directors), long scarves, heavy bracelets, medallions and headphones.

Well-dressed gentlemen

Harold Macmillan (Earl Stockton)	Ronnie Corbett
Robert MacDougall	Ted Heath
David Steel	Patrick Moore
Sir Peter Hall	Roger Moore
Michael Heseltine	Brian Moore

Not so well-dressed gentlemen

George Best

Leon Brittan (C & A's Man of the Year)

Terry McCann

Dickie Davis

Ron Atkinson (he's doing to jewellery
what Nobby Stiles did to football)

Dustin Hoffman

Elton John

Jimmy Savile

Barry Manilow

Lord Hailsham

A gentleman's club

A gentleman needs a club – a base where he can be contacted and a drink can be had after hours. Just as Tory politicians need the Carlton (annual subscription £255), successful actors and barristers need the Garrick (subscription £275), or the unemployed need Annabelle's, so the likes of me need the Winchester Club (annual subscription by negotiation and reference).

References are important. At the Carlton they want to know about your school or occupation. At the Winchester somebody will say: 'I'll vouch for him, he's one of our own.'

There are differences, of course. At the Winchester, every year somebody has it away with the Loan Club kitty. They don't do that at the Carlton – not even in the Junior one.

Many of the applicants fill in their membership forms by writing 'Occupation: shepherd' (or deep sea diver). The motto of the club is: NEVER PAY THE RIGHT PRICE. NEVER GIVE YOUR RIGHT NAME. AND KEEP SHTUM.

The atmosphere is social, relaxing and anecdotal. You'll see expert hoisters (shoplifters) swapping stories with blaggers and con men. You can always get hold of an American Express card, a hooky cheque book or even two thousand cards for the *Mirror* £1-million bingo prize.

Members are not into dominoes, darts or discussing their allotments or fishing. The milieu is one of cheerful villainy. They'll tell you about last week's bank robbery or somebody else plotting next week's bank robbery. All in good fun and certainly no question about violence.

Although I am the chairman of the Wine Committee (Hirondelle is always a winner and nothing too old), our mine host is big Dave. He's a bit like the parish priest. A man of wisdom, shrewdness and nothing goes further than this, my old son.

It was old Dave who invented the name Winchester Club. Apparently, in his youth – and in all accounts he was a bit of a Jack the lad – he had a close encounter with the judiciary. His probation officer was a Wykehamist, who are well known for doing good things (the salt of the middle-class earth, in fact). Unfortunately, some of the Wykehamists are also well known for 'kiting', that is, tendering dodgy cheques. He was nicked himself. Dave started his club, naming it after his ex-probation officer, and when he came out Dave gave him a job as a pot-man (a lowly position, but beggars can't be choosers). Three months later he was dipping in the till and Dave gave him the elbow. That's your Wykehamist for you. But it's a touching story.

Dave is a kindly and generous man, almost to a fault. Often a member will come in with a small package and say: 'Bung that in the fridge for me.' And as Dave has told me many times: 'That old fridge has had a brace of pheasant, six Cartier gold watches, a fistful of dollars, uncut diamonds, Mont Blanc pens, three Smith & Wesson .38s, a Walther PPK, a blue and white porcelain flask (Ming dynasty, 15th century, valued about fifty grand), and Lord Nelson's glass eye, three times, inside it. The old fridge has got a story to tell. The only thing you can't get out of it is ice cubes.'

I fondly recall that day when a member appeared with a toucan, a species of the bird family. He'd picked it up in Harrods' pet shop, largely because it was available. 'Bung it in the fridge for me,' he said to Dave. It was too big though. But another member bought the toucan from him. He said he was going fishing.

What is a bubble?

You might be feeling confused, wondering when to describe someone as a bubble*. Can you describe Socrates as a bubble, for example? Or Plato or Aristotle or the likes of Homer? No, you can't. But my good friend Nick, who runs the dry cleaners' down the road, *is* a bubble. That doesn't mean disrespect – a bubble is just a simple term of description for a Greek.

It seems to me that your ancient Greeks – Olympians and Spartans and the others – were a different breed. They had a classic profile. In fact, they looked more like English people. Have you had a look at their statues – you wouldn't call them bubbles, would you? Can you imagine Socrates running a take-away kebab caff? No, Athens was the cradle of civilisation, the nursery of art, architecture and drama. Obviously, Greece has changed, just like us all. You drop into the Parthenon Social Club in Tufnell Park and you won't hear a lot about Greek drama and statues. All they do is play darts.

---

* bubble = bubble and squeak = Greek

Never a debtor nor a lender be — well, at least don't lend.

A to Z of ethnic London

TO THE NORTH
(farmers, miners, tripeland and Scotchmen)

EAST FINCHLEY
(Italian waiters)

GOLDERS GREEN
(more Jews than Tel Aviv)

HOLLOWAY
(the free Irish state)

STANMORE
(Roman settlement)

HAMPSTEAD
(the highest concentration of *Guardian* readers)

KENTISH TOWN
(for people who can't afford a house in Canonbury)

SOUTHALL
(Vindaloo land)

KILBURN
(Guinness on tap)

SWISS COTTAGE
(downtown Vienna)

WORMWOOD SCRUBS
(where all your friends meet - eventually)

£ $ $
£ PARK LANE
(Saudi Arabia)
£ $ £ $

WARREN STREET
(where all good motors start and end)

SOHO
(porn, French cooking, Maltese ponces and strippers)

WHITE CITY

GERRARD STREET
(Chinatown)

QUEEN'S PARK RANGERS

SOUTH KEN
KNIGHTSBRIDGE ←→ BELGRAVIA
(rich and nice people)

EARLS COURT
(kangaroo valley)

CHELSEA
(land of the rich and the young)

THE OVAL

STAMFORD BRIDGE

THE WINCHESTER CLUB
(British posession)

BATTERSEA
(for people who can't afford a house in Chelsea)

BRIXTON
(and you know what happens there)

CLAPHAM
(for people who can't afford a house in Battersea)

FULHAM FOOTBALL GROUND

BALHAM
(for people who can't afford a house in Clapham)

PUTNEY

WANDSWORTH PRISON

UPPER TOOTING
(gawd knows what happens there)

THE SURREY ALPS

APACHE LAND

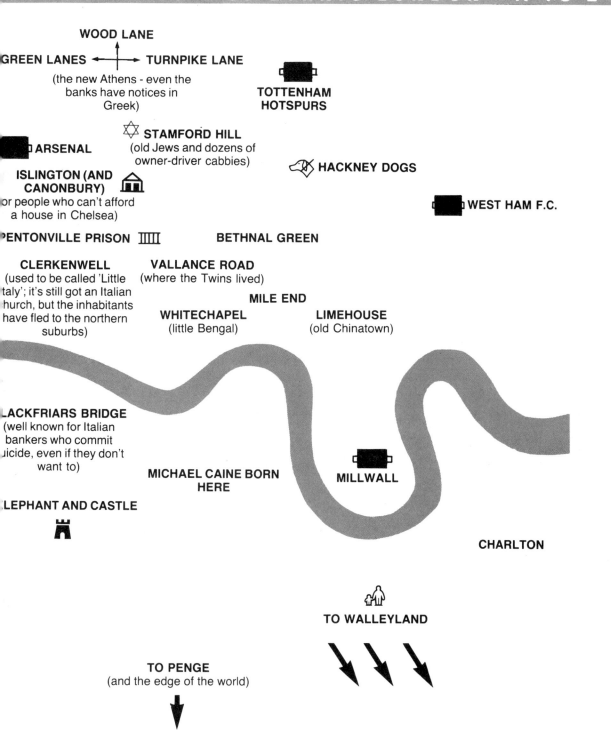

WOOD LANE

GREEN LANES ←→ TURNPIKE LANE

(the new Athens - even the
banks have notices in
Greek)

TOTTENHAM
HOTSPURS

STAMFORD HILL
(old Jews and dozens of
owner-driver cabbies)

ARSENAL

HACKNEY DOGS

ISLINGTON (AND
CANONBURY)

or people who can't afford
a house in Chelsea)

WEST HAM F.C.

PENTONVILLE PRISON

BETHNAL GREEN

CLERKENWELL
(used to be called 'Little
taly'; it's still got an Italian
hurch, but the inhabitants
have fled to the northern
suburbs)

VALLANCE ROAD
(where the Twins lived)

MILE END

WHITECHAPEL
(little Bengal)

LIMEHOUSE
(old Chinatown)

LACKFRIARS BRIDGE
(well known for Italian
bankers who commit
uicide, even if they don't
want to)

MICHAEL CAINE BORN
HERE

MILLWALL

LEPHANT AND CASTLE

CHARLTON

TO WALLEYLAND

TO PENGE
(and the edge of the world)

What is a walley?

In my youth a 'walley' was a pickled cucumber or large gherkin – an object similar to that part of the masculine anatomy.

Nowadays a walley is a person. You can always spot one because he's wearing a pair of Hush Puppies, a fisherman-knit jersey and a Casio digital watch. He drives a second-hand Datsun Cherry and his big night out is a couple of pints of real ale, a pipeful of St Bruno and a German film.

Walleys are sometimes confused with civilians or 'punters'. Civilians use public transport. They go to Tesco's, do the pools and pay their bills. They're the salt of the earth. They write letters to the newspapers and they like dogs, cats and budgies. They always remember birthdays and they're into do-it-yourself, cleaning cars on Sundays, chest freezers, videos, security and relatives. They're punctual, hard-working and truthful. They're always witnessing accidents and crimes and being commended by judges. People like me sell them hooky TV sets, videos, hi-fis, food blenders, thermal socks, insurance policies and guaranteed second-hand motors used by careful lady owners. They're honest to a fault.

And where would I be without them?

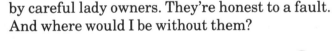

How to recognise a villain

Rogues, rascals and scallywags come in all different sizes and shapes. Not that I know these kinds of people. I meet them, but I'm not one of them.

Physical crime is a young man's occupation. To rob and steal you have to be fit because at any minute you have to have it on your heels. There is also the wear and tear of the nervous system. As in all stress professions, this becomes a daily hazard.

There is a rigid structure in villainy. On one side you've got con men, armed robbers, safebreakers, burglars and hoisters (in that order) and on the other side are the gangsters.

Gangsters thieve off thieves. They're the kings of the jungle. Some of them are lovely people. They're into money, hitting people, violence (they're partial to the old army bayonet) and, occasionally, killing people. They also like charities, helping old boxers, faded

RTHUR

57

showbusiness personalities and children. They get their money from fraudulent companies, drinking clubs, wine bars, drugs, pop festivals. And the threat of violence to all the other thieves.

It's a family business, gangsterism. They've got lots of brothers and cousins, and sons join the business.

They love talking about money and are conscious of brandnames. It has to be a Cartier or Rolex watch and they'll tell you the price, to the last penny (obviously, they didn't buy it). The shoes will be Gucci and the suit will be a Chester Barrie (or an expensive Italian one). But what they've got has to be shown. If you don't ask them they'll tell you. 'What's that, John?' 'That's an 18-carat gold toothpick on a gold chain, done by Cartier,' they'll say. And don't laugh. Gangsters have no sense of humour. Rough badinage, maybe, or even bandages, but don't take the piss.

How to tell a real lady

Well, for a start, my relationship with 'er indoors is none of your business; it's a personal, intimate and therefore a private matter. But I might just add that she's well trained, knows her place, keeps the gaff tidy, cooks a reasonable roast, Yorkshire pudding and two veg and she's as clean as a whistle. I think of her as a lady. By that I mean she's quiet and she wouldn't throw fag-ends in the grate. She wouldn't drink Mackeson's milk stout or even a Tequila Sunrise, and she'll always take off her gloves when eating. No bad language and she doesn't want to know about my business affairs. I think she's got a great life. She's got her little Metro, three weeks in Portugal with the kids, her *Cosmopolitan* and a daily woman. Her ideal day out is spent at Brent Cross shopping centre or a couple of hours window-shopping at Harrods (anything she fancies I can always get hold of for half-price any time).

She's certainly *not* a feminist – one of those birds who drinks pints of bitter, organises petitions and writes letters to the *Guardian*.

A real lady has a sense of moderation. That means she doesn't wear climbing boots or extravagant hair styles or carry a handbag that looks like a rucksack. Ladies wear Laura Ashley frocks and have matching wallpaper in the living room. They can read novels – or even write them. People are always surprised when women succeed in commerce, industry, science or sport because they're not naturals. Though I must say, I've never met a lady shifting a BMW in Warren Street or selling a second-hand Skoda, and that's not a knack it's an art. The qualities I'm looking for in a woman are:

The modesty of Princess Diana
The figure of Bo Derek
The legs of Cyd Charisse
The eyes of Sophia Loren
The ruthlessness of Mrs Thatcher
Respect for parents like Princess Michael
The intelligence of Barbara Windsor
The wealth of Jackie Onassis

I hope I've got these in the right order?

Eating out your heart

I know my food. But one of the hazards of eating out is confronting foreign waiters who despise the English punters.

The top of the list is the French, who think they invented food. The Italians are friendly almost to the point of being family. Give them a chance and they're chatting up the ladies in the party. Indians would rather be serving half an ounce of Old Holborn and the *Sun* in their corner shop, and the Chinese – well, you can't read them, can you? They've got Gerrard Street and Maggie's given them Hong Kong, so why not Dawes Road tomorrow? That's what's uppermost in their minds.

The Englishman doesn't want to be a waiter, even if the alternative means standing on his feet and queuing up to get his Giro. We're not natural lackeys. Look at these Job Centres – they're hardly striving, pulsating centres of enterprise. The English worker is a quiet man, yeoman stock. He'd rather stay in his kip instead of putting on a T-shirt or bow tie and serving some bloke who's the same as him.

Look at British Railways. Their waiters are English. And they spill the soup even when the train's in the station.

I go to many restaurants and at least twelve times a year I go to various functions. You're dipping in your pocket for a worthy cause like Micky Duff's Anglo-American Sporting Club dinner and a boxing 'do' at the Hilton (which is the most worthier cause – Micky or the Hilton?). Or it's a benefit dinner for a second-rate footballer or a variety star of yesteryear, and the Stable Lads Boxing Night (Grosvenor House), where you can scoff your prawn cocktail and watch several midgets hitting each other.

With my long experience of noshing out I would suggest that you follow my simple rules.

SIMPLE RULES FOR EATING OUT

1 Anything that's got a sauce on it, reject it.

2 The *pomme frite* is not the same as a chip. The chip has a substance, particularly the soggy bit in the middle.

3 Order what you know.

4 If they can't grill a decent steak they can't make a Coq au Vin.

5 If the bread costs extra, go somewhere else.

6 If a waiter is really friendly he's anticipating a large tip. Well, if he's that friendly why doesn't he give you a rebate?

7 Avoid those restaurants where the waiter has to explain each item of the menu, like: 'Thinly cut small ribs of succulent West of England spring lamb marinated in wild thyme, hazelnuts, Tuscany currants, hothouse apricots, two tablespoonfuls of Peter Dominic red wine, diced with New Forest mushrooms and baby Harlow New Town carrots, pine kernels and a liberal dollop of farmhouse Jersey cream, etc., etc.' What you've got there is lamb chops.

The Arthur Daley work-out

Do not abuse your body and your organs. God gave you a machine – not perfect, but good enough. It's up to you to keep it in good nick. Think of it as your other and most expensive asset – the motor. It has to be serviced, hasn't it? And sometimes the big end goes.

There is an epidemic of fitness and it's catching. Jane Fonda, Raquel Welch and even the darts players are having a go. Can you imagine the Crafty Cockney or Jocky Wilson explaining their regime for fitness? They've usually got a fag in one hand and a pint of lager in the other one, and their biggest exercise is walking from the chalk-mark to the dart board. Daley Thompson can do that in one leap, blindfolded.

There is an epidemic of fitness. Some of them are developing their triceps, others are developing their property. I want to give you some hints. We executives have to be fit. I don't sit behind a desk – we're ducking and diving. At any minute you have to jump into the motor and drive to a car auction or meet an unsatisfied footballer trying to off-load his complimentary tickets. The man with ten microwave ovens wants a quick decision and you probably have to hump them to the motor instantly. You have to be alert not only to handle muggers but also to fend off aggressive VAT Inspectors too.

I don't want you to pump iron or do two hundred push-ups when you're reading the *Financial Times* of a morning. Some of my contemporaries have had enough of weight-lifting, largely because where they were there was nothing else to do.

My work-out is simple – NO JOGGING. The mature man doesn't want to know about running and being savaged by dogs.

When you get up breathe deeply. Open the window and gulp some of that fresh air. Two minutes – you don't want to get a chill. If you have a static bicycle (I have forty of them in my lock-up, £55 a throw, and you'll never get a better one), don't go mad or you'll be knackered before you start.

I'm a great believer in Dynamic Tension. Do you remember old Charles Atlas? Obviously you're not going to get sand in your eyes walking down the Fulham Road, unless, of course, some Irish labourer is mixing up his cement for yet another conversion. Press your hands together – as if you've lost a cockle on a stone racing certainty – until you feel the sweat in your palms. That's dynamic tension.

You should be burning off calories by nervous energy – picking up the rag-and-bone or flexing your wrist muscles as you tot up the day's takings on your calculator.

The mysterious East offers us a new lifestyle. I've dabbled in yoga. You have to be fit in India what with the famines, floods and natural disasters. I often discuss these topics with Mr Patel, my local grocer, as he smokes his filter-tip. (The way he smokes them I think he's been sponsored by John Player.) You have a wander in Southall . . . they're busy people, up in the morning to open their newsagent shops. The kids have done a full day's work before they've gone to school. You don't see Indians in the Job Centre. That's probably why Richard Attenborough likes them.

THE DUCKER'S AND DIVER'S DIET

Breakfast: nothing wrong with a couple of cups of Sergeant's Brew. Two pieces of toast with Marmite will set you up for the morning. There is an optional cup of tea (no biccies) at eleven. This will sustain you till you get a livener at about 12.30 – two glasses of carbohydrate-free German lager and then you can get into the serious stuff, a large vodka and slimline.

Lunch: a sandwich in a pub (thinly spread marge on white bread; you ain't going to get butter anyway). Ham, cheese (no pickle) or beef, two leaves of lettuce, one tomato and one gherkin.

Tea: no tea.

Dinner: I like an early dinner, otherwise it interferes with your evening work and socialising. Steak (no chips), a few sprouts and peas and half a baked potato. No sweet. Black coffee and a teeny brandy.

HOW TO REDUCE YOUR ALCOHOLIC INPUT

This is part of your diet. How to be social without saying 'I'm on a dry.' Like with most tricks you need the help of a second party. Explain to the barman that you are trying to pace yourself, and that your first drink will be a vodka and slimline. When another colleague calls a round you give a nod to the barman. He'll top up the glass with slimline. The next one will be vodka and slimline and the next just slimline, and so on. With a reasonable school and a session of four hours the money mounts up. You can collect your dough later and give a couple of bob to the barman. The beauty of this is you don't offend friends, you cut drinking by half and you've got money in your pocket as well.

How to fail successfully and be rich

Every Englishman dreams of being his own guv'nor. These days we're a nation of Pakistani shopkeepers. Your ordinary Englishman doesn't want to know about getting up at half past five and shuffling copies of the *Sun* and *Mirror*. Corner shops are hard work and who needs that?

A man like myself – a thrusting entrepreneur, an impresario of commerce – knows that getting a crust ain't easy. Alas, there are some dishonest dealers who try to short-circuit our private enterprise system. The kind of people who would agree with the thesis of 'getting on your bike' with the proviso that first you nick a bike. And if you nick enough of them you don't have to go anywhere except to the bank.

These wicked people give a bad name to the competitive society. What they do is start companies with the deliberate aim of failing.

The principals of the organisation are going to cop bundles but the creditors are in shtuk. This is called a 'long firm'.

To float a 'long firm' is about as complicated as starting a real company. You need capital, bank accounts, references, an accountant and book-keeper, premises – at least a warehouse – and a hard-working staff, including salesmen, plus a sense of adventure. You even have to do some research on sussing out the loophole in the market.

A favourite market is the one of electrical appliances. Easy to move, easy to sell at a certain price. Toiletries are good, so are furniture, kitchen units, tools, carpets, clothes.

Let's assume that we're going to start a wholesale domestic electric appliances company.

You've sussed the area and there is no other wholesaler within three miles. A friendly estate agent has offered you a short-lease warehouse – the GLC often has premises.

A friend has a daughter who's just finished her graphics course at the local art school. For £150 she'll design the stationery, cards and invoices. You'll be amazed how many respectable people would like to be company directors. They'll be a front because you don't want to have your name on the letterhead.

The bank manager is delighted that you've opened an account of, say, £40,000, and within twelve minutes you've become great mates. Your company is marketing a new revolutionary German hairdryer and you'd be delighted if the manager's wife would accept our complimentary item. (It's been on the market for a year but the bank manager's wife isn't going to refuse simply because it's *not* a revolutionary hairdryer, is she?) You will meet representatives from Philips, Zanussi, Hitachi, GEC and Braun and give them orders. They'll write to your bank and they'll get a letter from them saying that 'AD Products & Co. are good for £5,000 [the value of the order] and the principals are known to our branch.'

The company pays its bills on the dot. And the orders get bigger. You're selling well, largely because your prices are keen (say, thirty per cent less than any other firm can offer). In fact you're losing money. A good accountant would say you're on the road to bankruptcy. But your accountant isn't good, he's crooked.

Credit begets credit. AD Products is booming. Your best customers are retailers; you're offering them items they can't refuse. And the public at large are getting incredible bargains. You're the most popular man in the manor. You're putting in eight hours a day – it's almost like working. Any minute somebody's going to put you up for the Chamber of Commerce.

It takes six months. The man from Philips is delighted with your bumper order. And the man from GEC (and one from Hitachi) has given you a nice drink as well. 'I don't know how you do it,' he says. And you're not going to tell him.

Now you've got about a month or six weeks. The warehouse is crammed with vacuums, fridges, blenders, coffee machines, hair-dryers and everything else you've ordered. You and your helpers are working like good 'uns. You're selling for silly money but it's all coming to you. The invoices are ignored and you don't even read the reminders. It's robbery of course, but it's not like stealing in the night or jumping out with balaclavas and pickaxe handles. And the tame directors are unlikely to go to prison.

I wonder how many Cash and Carry companies have been started with stock from a moody long firm exercise? All right, I was just thinking.

Now the warehouse is empty. The remaining stock you couldn't sell has been moved to a dozen lock-ups wherever. The bank account has been closed. Correspondence piles up. They don't even pay the telephone bill. A VAT Inspector is sniffing around but by that time you're on your early holiday in Marbella with a hold-all containing £300,000. You've worked for it, haven't you?

Note: Are you interested in a German-made revolutionary hair-dryer? I'm giving 'em away.

Harrods is better for hoisting

Hoisting is not the same as shoplifting. When you hear that a female East European javelin-thrower has been nicked for taking a Crimplene jumper from Marks & Spencer *that's* shoplifting. But if you hear that somebody's had it away with ten dozen cashmere sweaters from Harrods – that's hoisting. See, it's a different game.

I have to explain that I meet hoisters in the course of my business day. I don't do it meself. They have a simple philosophy: if you have to nick, nick the best. You're never going to see a professional hoister in Marks & Spencer or the British Home Stores, excellent institutions as they are. The hoister goes to Harrods and Liberty and then Peter Jones, the Army & Navy, D. H. Evans, Heals, Maples and the like. If they've got a special order they'll go to Habitat – but only for the younger set.

Harrods know what's going on. But what can they do? The exclusive clientele of Harrods don't want to meet security men every five yards. The charm of the shop is that you can relax, browse, chat to the educated sales staff, exchange your dollars or yen, buy your grouse or lose your handbag. You don't want to hear cries of 'Thief! Stop him!' every two minutes. I've got a feeling that the staff recognise every top hoister in London, but they probably think that they're regular customers. It's that kind of store, innit?

The hoister is a professional. He only goes to work when the pickings are good. He's not interested in two leather jackets – he swipes the whole rack-full.

There is a specialist hoister who will actually take orders. You could furnish a flat or replenish your wardrobe from this specialist.

This country of ours is blessed by a rich and colourful language. But funnily enough there is no apposite word for this specialist. From my contacts across the water there is such a word – they call him a 'booster'. I offer it to the alternative linguists.

Now, one of the hazards of buying in the free economy is you don't always get what you ask for. The price is always half the retail price. Being a hi-fi buff you order superb Bang & Olufsen equipment. But your man appears and says they're fresh out of B & O gear but he's got you the new technological breakthrough from South Korea and 'Stand on me, they'll all want them in a couple of months.' Or you've ordered a new sofa. You actually went into Maples and picked the colour and even jotted down the order number, just in case there's some confusion.

A week later your man is on the doorstep and you say: 'I asked you to get Pale Polar Blue; I actually saw it in the shop.'

'They don't do it any more,' your man says. 'That was the last one. They had a lot of complaints about Pale Polar Blue. What you've got here is Iceland Grey, which I personally think is a better colour.'

Now you're in a quandary. The man's done you a right favour, price-wise, but you've got a hookey South Korean hi-fi set which you've never heard of and a sofa in a colour which you don't fancy. You're still muttering about Pale Polar Blue and he's saying: 'Well, are you calling me a liar?' and 'I ain't gonna exchange it, am I?'

Of course, you're not going to call him a liar. That's no way to conduct business.

I'm afraid it's the usual British customer relationship. They haven't got it; they can't get it; there's a strike at the docks; and if they *can* get it there's going to be a long waiting list.

No wonder the country's going down the drain.

On the carpet

This is a simple exercise in salesmanship. Naturally it's not something which I've tried myself but some of my colleagues have told me about it. The ingredients needed for this are as follows:

1 middle-class home-owner (usually the wife)
2 one so-called Persian carpet
3 two men wearing white coats or overalls and a reasonable skill in acting
4 a van
5 time limit: 15 minutes

The idea is to sell a Persian carpet (made in Belgium) to a know-it-all punter.

Two men knock on the door. They seem slightly nervous and they don't understand the commodity they are trying to sell. One bloke is looking over his shoulder. The other would address the punter thus:

'Would you be interested in a carpet? It's really nice, patterned, they call them Persian—

His partner: 'Bokhara . . . or something like that.'

The other one: 'That's it . . . See, we've been working on the new estate, the luxury flats down the road . . . [and indeed a new block of flats has been completed] And this carpet was in the show flat and the guv'nor said we could have it because it's secondhand – I mean, nothing wrong with it . . .'

The punter/housewife's reaction is: 'These scoundrels have pinched it. I know more about Persian rugs than them because I've read *House & Gardens* and secondhand Persian rugs are just as expensive as the new ones. I'll spin them along and find out the price. I say, wouldn't it be rather dashing to buy a "hot" rug?'

Sixty per cent of home-owners would say 'No thank you.' The others are vaguely interested.

So the punter asks to see the carpet. The lads seem a bit concerned. The other one is still looking over his shoulder and his pal says: 'It's quite big. I don't want to bring it in unless you're interested . . .'

And the punter says: 'I've got to see it, haven't I?'

The bloke says you can see it in the van. And of course now the punter *knows* it's stolen, but there's no harm in having a dekko, eh?

They open the van door and indeed the carpet is Persian or similar and it's rather nice, and I wonder how much they'll ask for it?

Within three minutes the lads carry the carpet into the house, one of them muttering to himself and still looking over his shoulder.

Now they're in the sitting room and the carpet looks a treat. The punter is impressed and asks how much it is.

'You can have it for £200,' one says.

It's a bit steep. But the other one, who seems so nervous, says to his mate: 'I'd be quite happy to have £150.'

The housewife tells them that she doesn't have that kind of cash in the house. And the one who was doing the talking says they'll take a cheque.

[*Note:* they only work during banking hours and they assume that the punter's bank is in the area.]

For the first time the housewife has certain misgivings. She'll have to phone her husband. She wants to keep the lads in her sight just in case they nick the carriage clock on the mantelpiece. Now it's old Giles on the rag-and-bone. He's not all that keen but Lavinia knows a thing about carpets and even old Giles realises that a largish Persian carpet sells for between £700 and two grand.

Lavinia writes the cheque and drops a couple of remarks about 'I hope it's not stolen or anything!' Or [*little laugh*] 'Will we have a visit from the Old Bill?' (She's heard that from television.) And the lads reassure her and they're off to the bank before Lavinia thinks about it again. Fifteen minutes, no more.

The interesting thing about the exercise is that when Lavinia and Giles got up that morning the last thing they thought about was buying a Persian carpet made in Belgium.

If they'd walked down the High Street they could've seen a similar carpet priced at £65. But they wouldn't go into those down-market shops. For several weeks they'll be telling their friends about their bargain – even more, how Lavinia tricked the simple artisans who didn't know the value of the article. Several months later they'll meet a friend who bought a similar carpet and another friend (who knows about carpets) says you've been done, and two years later the carpet disintegrates. All I say is, 'Where's the harm?'

How to lease a council flat near Sloane Square and make some money

Have you ever thought of leasing a council flat near Sloane Square and making some money?

Do 'civilians' need a good postal address? Wouldn't they be happier living in a high-rise tower in Deptford near their place of work or a handy DHSS office? I throw it in for discussion.

There are little oases of council property – converted period houses – in desirable areas like Chelsea, Hampstead, Bayswater, Islington and even in the *outré* parts of Southwark, Wapping and Hackney.

By word of mouth and money of fist you can collect a portfolio of attractive flats. For example, you hear that a certain party is having domestic strife. He's gone off with a betting shop settler or she's scarpered with an Italian waiter. The kids are in care or they're living with their gran. The sole surviving tenant is strapped for dough. At this point, you appear and offer two or three grand, in readies. You take the rent book, and a couple of likely lads with two gallons of Dulux Brilliant White and a roller will refurbish the whole gaff. Three posters from the Tate Gallery and furniture of the 'Maples-and-die' variety and you're in business.

You have to pay the rent (say £35 p.w.) on the dot. Obviously, you have to forge the signature of the council tenant but that ain't hard, is it? You need a responsible private tenant now. Go for company lets or visiting 'academics', six-month leases and you're asking for £175 or £225 per week. And you're going to be a perfect landlord. Any repairs will be done promptly, and you'll be nice and polite to the neighbours.

A little tip: sometimes you can spot a council conversion by the door furniture – they use standard letterboxes, knockers and bells, in brushed chrome. Replace them with brass (£24). If other tenants or neighbours ask why, you say it's a new council policy – they want their houses to look like private houses.

They'll be knocked out. Nobody wants to live in a council property anyway.

I am assuming a two-bedroom, k & b, one recep., in a decent street.

Profit and loss account of leasing a
council flat and making money

The first year:

LOSS		PROFIT	
Paying off tenant:	£2,500		
Decoration	400		
Furniture	800		
Coffee machine (for foreigners)	20		
Brass knocker and letterbox	24		
Posters	8		
Rent to council £35 p.w.	1,820		
Rates (per annum)	200	Rent £225 per week =	11,700
	5,760		11,700

The second year:

LOSS		PROFIT	
Sundry repairs	£200	Rent	£11,700
		Tax	nil
	£200		£11,700

Profit in cold blood (two years):   £17,440

You can do this for about five years. Eventually the council may suss it out. But there's always a happy ending. Whoever is renting the flat will be rehoused by the council anyway.

How to while away the hours if you're Jack the lad

Here is a typical day in the life of Jack the Lad. Your villain gets up late. The only time to see a villain in the early morning is when he's going home after a hard night's boozing or a bit of skulduggery. The early morning is a no-go time zone. Since recorded history there is no case of a milkman being hijacked.

Jack the Lad gets up between 11 and noon. Breakfast is traditional: bacon, eggs, fried bread and lots of tea. They don't drink coffee and they're not all that crazy about Rice Krispies and the like. Ablutions are leisurely, with plenty of after-shave (and it must be expensive, e.g. Ted Lapidus, Roche, Yves St. Lawrence Corner. Old Spice is for civilians). Surprisingly, Jack the Lad lives with his mum – until he's ready to move into his common-law wife's little flat.

You won't see a lot of Jack the Lads in restaurants at lunchtime. Tough guys don't have lunch, unless they're doing a bit of business. About two o'clock they go to their favourite pub to meet the chaps. It has to be a special pub, usually run by one of the chaps or a real 'character' who understands their little ways.

There is a Daley Law that says 'two hundred people run every profession'. There are two hundred brain surgeons in the country and they all know each other. There are two hundred writers who really get a living out of writing, two hundred chairmen who are successful in business, and two hundred taxi-drivers who know each other and get by. It's the same in villainy: two hundred men get by, the top of the profession. To become one of the two hundred you have to be rated and respected.

All the top criminals know each other. They wear the same kind of clothes, the same kind of Tom on their wrists and more gold on their chests than Daley Thompson. Jack the Lad likes Bacardi and coke, vodka with anything, German wine, champagne (Moët & Chandon, and Dom Perignon after a tickle) and the occasional lager. You hardly ever see them drinking a pint of real ale, light and bitter or red wine.

After the pub there is a natural progression to the afternoon drinking club. Some of them forsake this pleasure for 'creeping

around', which means sussing out a likely bank or office or depot, or cruising the salubrious environs of the metropolis to spot a handy and vulnerable villa or mansion.

In the club big rounds will be called for, phonecalls made to bookmakers who don't take tax and endless anecdotes told about failed crimes and conspiracies. At about six o'clock Jack the Lad has to 'shoot off' and meet his second cousin, who happens to be working for a security firm these days.

He'll go home and see his mum and have a meal. Jack the Lad who lives alone won't cook for himself. He'll go to his favourite Italian restaurant. They don't fancy French cuisine or kebabs or even Indian – it's always Italian.

They don't go to the theatre or classical concerts but they like a film and they want to see a new film before anybody else sees it. You certainly get some brownie points for going to the première or to a private screening and a bonus for being the first person in your group for having the pirate video.

They do like going to the Hilton and the Grosvenor for dinner and boxing, or dancing at Stringfellows or Tramp and chatting to the drunken footballers. The Jack the Lad likes to know a few celebrities, the odd actor and actress, pop musicians and sporting personalities.

But they're more comfortable gambling and drinking to the early hours. They don't go to ordinary casinos because they don't offer their favourite games and real action. They like to be with their own so they go to a spieler – a private gambling club. The games are kalooki, dice and high-stakes poker. Later, Jack the Lad might pull one of the hostesses. At about six o'clock he'll be back at home. It's a full day for him but doesn't do a lot for the balance of payments.

Is violence justified?

I abhor violence. I abhor all those little soccer hooligans, muggers, wife-beaters, husband-beaters, louts, yobbos, armed robbers, terrorists, urban guerrillas, bully-boys, gangsters, bother-boys and people who resort to fisticuffs to solve arguments.

I am for law and order. (Not *too* much law, mind you.) But what can a man do when he's been turned over? There are occasions when disputes are beyond litigation. After the mandatory final demands, solicitor's letters and pleas of 'You're taking diabolical liberties, old son,' what happens next? I'll tell you what: he gets a spanking, or even a smack or a clout.

The rule is clear: if a man does violence to my pocket he's going to know about it.

I'm not asking for him to be hung, drawn and quartered but merely for a reasonable retribution. I mean, Clint Eastwood has done it dozens of times.

Spare the rod and you've got a naughty boy. A smack with a ruler on a bare leg or six of the best and they know what's going on.

If they've got a reasonable excuse then we sit down and discuss it. I'm not a bloodthirsty man. Nor am I suggesting that the Gas Board should adopt the policy because you're a bit short one month, or that the Inland Revenue should send in a couple of heavies to collect your back tax. (Mind you, some of their letters are very threatening.)

Obviously, I'd rather have the money but, if not, I need satisfaction. I have to encourage the others. If one punter can get away with it what about the others? They'll all start to knock me. You must understand that there are people who get a living out of knocking honest traders. They need a wigging-off, don't they? And having got hold of the culprit, at what point do you extract his debt?

How much claret equals the original sum? Has the spanking settled the bill? These are the kind of ethical problems we discuss at my club during the wee small hours.

There is a school of thought which says that the punishment is but a penalty. The original debt still stands. He stills owes you. Another school suggests that the hammering is a fulfilment of the offence. Given a reasonable time span you may now do business with each other again.

Young Terence, who is surprisingly squeamish about these matters, says the debtor has given full expiation but you should have known he was a wrong 'un from the start.

Television

MY FAVOURITE ALL-TIME TV PROGRAMMES

1 *Sergeant Bilko*
2 *This is Your Life*
3 *Angels*
4 *Law and Order*
5 *The Prisoner*
6 *The World About Us*
7 *The Money Programme*
8 *Tomorrow's World*
9 *Antiques Road-show*
10 *Dixon of Dock Green*

... AND THE VERY WORST

1 *Gideon of the Yard*
2 *The Sweeney*
3 *The Bill*
4 *Z-Cars*
5 *Softly, Softly*
6 *The Gentle Touch*
7 *Juliet Bravo*
8 *Starsky and Hutch*
9 *Hill Street Blues*
10 *Police 5*

. . . and that's where you get your violence. You switch on the box and you'll see coppers driving powerful motors chasing suspects in their Cortinas in the empty streets of inner London or wherever. They bash into parked cars or handy lamp-posts and they always get the right man – a nasty looking bloke, who never shaves. And they're a bit handy with the shooters, aren't they? Look at that Starsky, jumping out of windows. And that Reagan with his grubby anorak, lord mayoring all over the place. They are hardly an example for our younger citizens. And do they get the right man? Have a look at those brick walls in the city and you'll see graffiti proclaiming:

'George Huggins is Innocent'
'Free the Kentish Town Twelve'
'A Fair Trial for the Peckham Rye 37'
'My dogma was run over by my karma'
or 'Kill the Pigs' or 'P.C. Bloggins is Bent'.

You get the feeling that half of the prison population shouldn't even be in there.

Those TV coppers look like pop musicians and now you see real coppers wearing the same kind of gear. That's not right. In the old days you knew where you were: villains wore double-breasted suits and coppers wore sensible shoes and a Burberry or something similar. I blame the TV producers. There is far too much crime on the screen. After a day's hard graft I want to sit down and look at something interesting. For me, a series like *The World About Us* is informative and engrossing. With penguins and lost tribes in deepest Peru you know where you are.

MY FAVOURITE AUTHORS

1 Mario Puzo
2 Dick Francis
3 Hardy Amis (and his son)
4 Harold Robbins
5 Joyce James
6 Colin Welland (and he won the Oscar, didn't he?)

MY FAVOURITE ACTORS

1 Marlon Brando
2 David Niven
3 Jimmy Cagney
4 George Raft
5 Edward G. Robinson
6 Colin Welland

Helping the police with their enquiries

For a start, you may well ask why should I? Do they ever help me? Of course not.

I mean, they get good money, two white shirts, a tie and a decent pair of boots. What else do they want? Sometimes they have to work unsocial hours but against that they've got job satisfaction – like intimidating people, nicking them and then swearing your life away for you.

Don't get me wrong – I believe in law and order. I'd have those muggers, soccer hooligans, flying pickets, militant tendencies and even streakers on the Isle of Wight and if they get lippy I'd transport them to Devil's Island.

'Not me, guv'nor.'

What gets up my craw is the way they persecute the honest entrepreneur who's trying to get a crust, the buccaneers of the alternative economy, the men who are attempting to turn back the clock and make this country great again.

I have helped the Old Bill over the years. In fact, I gave them a microwave-oven for their canteen. And what did I get from it? I got a pull from Chisholm two weeks later when he was investigating a major theft at a famous kitchen utensils manufacturer's warehouse. That's what you get for helping the police with their enquiries.

Obviously I contribute to the Police Benevolent Fund from time to time. I gave £100 to a detective-constable – who will be nameless – only the other day. Did he actually share it with his colleagues? I don't know. And I also make it my business to know the name of the local bobby on the beat. Occasionally he'll get a drink. (See chapter 'What is a drink?') Does it help? Not really. It seems to me that they get not only younger, but stroppier.

Dogs still foul the pavement, Irish labourers spew on the corner and vandals snap the aerials off your motors. I had occasion to question Mr Plod about a neighbour's motor left bereft of alloy wheels (neatly done as well, bricked-up as if the thieves knew what they were doing. We're talking about a grand's-worth of wheels, you know.) And what did Mr Plod say to me? 'I thought you'd had 'em away, Mr Daley,' he said. That's what I mean when I say they're more stroppier. You wouldn't have had that from old Jack Warner, would you?

When you have your collar felt there is a certain routine. They say: 'You're nicked,' or 'I want to have a little chat with you,' or 'Let's go to the factory,'* or 'I've gotcha this time, sunshine.'

You say: 'Who? Me?' or 'You must be joking!' or 'I was at my auntie's that night.' You certainly *don't* say: 'You've done me bang to rights, guv'nor,' or 'It's a fair cop,' or 'I was waiting for this.'

There is a traditional repartee between the suspect and the investigating officer. He calls you by your Christian name and the suspect calls him by Mr. That's to show you that you're a naughty boy and he's a kindly but firm parent.

When you do go into the interview room you say, 'I want my brief.' And the officer says: 'Whatever for?' So you say, 'I know my rights.'

At this point the officer smirks at you. 'Rights?' he says. 'What rights? In this room I'm the only one with rights.'

You explain things like Magnus Carter and Habeas Corpus, Ester Rantzen, *Panorama* or Channel Four and he says: 'Are you being funny? Any more lip from you and I'm gonna throw the whole bleeding book at you. You'll see your brief when I decide . . . not before.'

At some point, the officer will say: 'You help me and I'll help you.'

What he really means is if you give him a full confession, plus a few names and a couple of grand for his piggy bank, he'll tip the nod to the judge and you'll be out in three years instead of seven. As I've said, 'Don't say nuffink.'

After twenty-three minutes the officer offers you a cigarette. They always do that, even if the suspect is a non-smoker. It's to show you that they're human and all-round decent guys.

Even if you're gasping for a fag you say, 'Mustn't . . . bad chest, dodgy heart. . . .' That's just to show them that you're in frail health

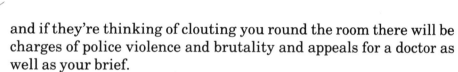

and if they're thinking of clouting you round the room there will be charges of police violence and brutality and appeals for a doctor as well as your brief.

After five hours (it's probably time for their tea) you say, 'I don't know what you're talking about. And that's straight, Mr Whatsisname.' This is your final word. It doesn't matter – they make it up anyway. It's called 'verbals' – evidence that you've said when being interviewed.

When helping the police with their enquiries the rule is: SILENCE IS GOLDEN, AND IT GETS YOU OUT OF TROUBLE AS WELL.

Incidentally, if you're innocent – that's a different thing, innit?

---

* The 'factory' is the local police station.

The Chisholm factor

Obviously, we need law and order but do we need the likes of Mr Chisholm? For several years now he has dogged my footsteps every day; even on his days off he dreams about me. And sometimes I dream about him.

Detective-Sergeant Chisholm (he failed his exams for Inspector two years ago) makes law and order into a personal obsession. Can you picture him? Those weasel eyes, the death-head smirk, his Marks and Spencer executive suit and his Escort with the go-faster stripes. (Yeah, I know his motor hasn't got go-faster stripes but it's all in the mind. He's an Escort-man aspiring for a Sierra XR4.)

Is he human? Some people say he's an honest copper. You can't corrupt him with cash or kind; he actually buys his own holiday airline tickets or his steak and chips in a basket. Surprisingly, I

Detective-Sergeant Chisholm on his better days is like a friendly member of the Gestapo.

have socialised with him, and after six large gins and tonics the man inside appears. The bold Chisholm is like an Old Testament prophet – an eye for an eye, a Cortina for a Cortina, a tooth for an arm, a leg and a foot, five years no less and no social workers in the box if he can prevent it.

Thus, Chisholm's Law is simple. 'I'm a *people* policeman,' he'll say after the six gins have done their toll. 'I consider my role as essentially preventive rather than detentive.' I haven't seen it myself – but that's his view. And if you top up his glass he'll plead for sympathy.

This is Chisholm, verbatim: 'Look at my environment . . . bloody tarts, pimps, grasses, muggers, drunks, rapists, transvestites, pedarists, wife-beaters, kiters, hoisters . . . what you might call an interesting cross-section of low-life. And I have to live in that environment. No wonder I'm cynical . . . After all that, to nick a decent, straightforward, honest-to-God bank robber is like a breath of good fresh air.'

The problem with Chisholm is he's got a highly developed sense of right and wrong, almost to the point of excess. But I say, let people get on with their lives without the Chisholms of this world probing into their affairs. He wants to be admired, respected and – can you believe it? – loved as well.

'It used to be like that in the old days,' says Chisholm. 'The lawman, the sheriff was the guv'nor in Dodge City or walking down the streets of Laredo. But you put John Wayne in a Ford Escort and he'll be spat at by kids with orange hair, abused by middle-class motorists, our ethnic friends will write letters to the GLC, pickets will throw lumps of concrete at him and even the dogs will try to bite his bumpers. It's no fun being a copper these days.'

Visiting friends in prison

Above all, be cheerful. You're out and he's in, so you should be cheerful.

Wear a good suit. He wants to remember what it's like outside. He looks like an air-raid warden from the war or a dodgy employee from British Rail. You owe him at least a nice piece of worsted or mohair and a hand-made silk tie.

He's likely to be depressed. In the conversation stakes you're going to make the running. Don't ask questions like:

1 Are they taking good care of you? (Yeah, I bet they are.)
2 Have you made any new friends? (Yeah, and some old ones he don't want to know.)
3 Are you sleeping well? Food all right? (No and no.)

Try and make him optimistic. Say things like: 'Look on the bright side, Charlie. Three more World Cups and you'll be out.'

Occasionally there will be a lull in the conversation. It's not like hospital where the visitor can get into the bunch of grapes. You have to realise that the prisoner is out of touch with real life. So you have to coax him into the discussion. Try and put yourself into his position. He hasn't got a lot to say really. Given the odd prison riot or 'Old Harry's been transferred to Broadmoor,' what can he say?

At some point or other he will deliver a soliloquy on his current obsessions. With not a lot to do in prison, obsessions are rife. It's usually about the quality of justice.

'I shouldn't even be here,' he says. 'They stitched me up, didn't they? I wasn't guilty . . . not in a million years. It was a fit-up. Where was the evidence? Nothing. It was all verbals – plus the super-grass. I mean, I don't even know the feller. I'll tell you one thing – I'll never use that brief again. Stand on me, Arthur, I was gutted. I mean, my brother had a contact on the jury. That's what you get these days . . . you can't trust anybody.'

You have to realise that ninety per cent who are arrested, charged and convicted are quite sure that the police didn't have enough evidence.

After this harangue against the judicial system it's all chitchat. 'I done four hundred push-ups in the gym the other day . . . my personal best,' he'll say. You'll tell him that the chaps have had a whip-round for his wife and family and oh, incidentally, Old Tony is up at the Bailey next month.

The longer they stay in the more they get accustomed to the routine. When you see him in about nine months he'll be making models of the *Royal Ark* in matchsticks and thinking of doing his O-levels. Such is the testimony of the reformative process of our prison system.

The noble art

This is my subject. The square ring, the smell of resin on the canvas, the ghosts of the past like Jem Belcher and Lord Byron (jotting down a poem with his right and sticking out a straight left at the same time) . . . It's a romantic game, the blood and the snot and the wonderful cries of 'Be first, son . . . be the guv'nor'. No wonder old Byron liked it and him with his bad leg.

I've studied the sport. I can tell you every world heavyweight champion since John L. Sullivan and a few before. And stand on me, things ain't what they used to be. Thank God Maggie's got the idea –

three and a half million on the rock 'n' roll and we'll get some real hungry fighters with a mean streak. No world champion scaled the heights with a Giro cheque in his back pocket.

Mind you, I blame a lot of it on the Labour government after the war and then Macmillan. The post-war babies were just too healthy and when they grew up they begat even healthier babies so now we're in the position of having taller and heavier young people. Our talent in the past was grooming superb flyweights. Now what have we got? Muscular heavyweights who can't move and all the little fellers want to be jockeys.

Just think about our heritage – Benny Lynch, Jackie Paterson, Peter Kane, Rinty Monaghan, Terry Allen, Dai Dower and plenty more. Do you realise that at this moment there are only *six* flyweights active in the whole country? They can't even fill the official rankings list. If you can find an eighteen-year-old midget who scales eight stone and hasn't got a gammy leg he's got a chance of being British champion after six months.

I know what I'm talking about. Ask any question about the noble art and I'll answer it. They'd love me to be on that TV programme with Agnes Magness, the Icelandic Scotchman and his famous electric chair.

Did you know that Max Schmelling won a world title when he was on the canvas? He was fouled by Jack Sharkey who regained the title in the return bout. And what about Nathan Mann, the Jewish heavyweight who was knocked out by Joe Louis in the Thirties (he wasn't really Jewish, he was a Catholic boy born in Sicily and his real name was Salvatore Margolese)? He was managed by that well known gangster, Dutch Shultz (whose real name was Arthur Flegenheimer), who thought it was time to have a Yiddisher heavyweight. All right, I know it's not the second law of thermo-nuclear dynamics, but it's interesting, innit?

Now they're trying to make boxing into show business. I think of the old days when the ringside seats were occupied by the cream of society wearing evening dress. You don't get that now. Even if you go to the National Sporting Club do (no shouting or applause during the rounds and no remarks like 'Play the white man!' because most of the fighters are black) at the Café Royale you won't see the aristocracy at play – just a couple of life peers, scrap-iron merchants and launderette owners and their accountants. Not a Lord Byron in the place.

The great outdoors

The reason why I stopped shooting is that it was getting too dangerous. You were supposed to shoot grouse or pheasant but with our syndicate you were never quite sure. High spirits, I suppose.

The members of the Winchester Club set are not natural participants of outdoors activities. The odd game of golf and that's it. You don't see rock-climbing gear in the corner or hear discussions about cycling, scuba diving, archery, tennis, beagling, tossing the caber, hunting, fishing or even polo.

I think it was the Kray twins who started the craze for shooting. Up to that time if somebody said 'We're going shooting' you assumed that they were off to the handiest branch of National Westminster. Suddenly they appeared in Barbour jackets, Irish thornproof suits or even smart Italian suits and loafers. For £20 a head they could vent all their frustrations by blowing off the heads of pigeons. There would be a remarkable array of armaments – Purdeys, Holland & Hollands, sawn-off shotguns, Smith & Wessons, Armalites and somebody had a bayonet as well.

None of them went to Scotland for the Glorious Twelfth; Essex seemed handier. There wasn't a Labrador between them, though Big Keith brought his Dobermann which was more of a savager than a retriever. It was Big Keith who ended the sound of gunfire. His tally one day was: two ducks, a grouse, a swan, the farmer's dog (he thought it was a fox), a 1981 Ford Cortina (a bloke having a picnic with his family) and a guy he had had a row with three months before.

The new craze is flying lessons. When you're a competent pilot you can flee to Marbella or even bomb the Royal Mint.

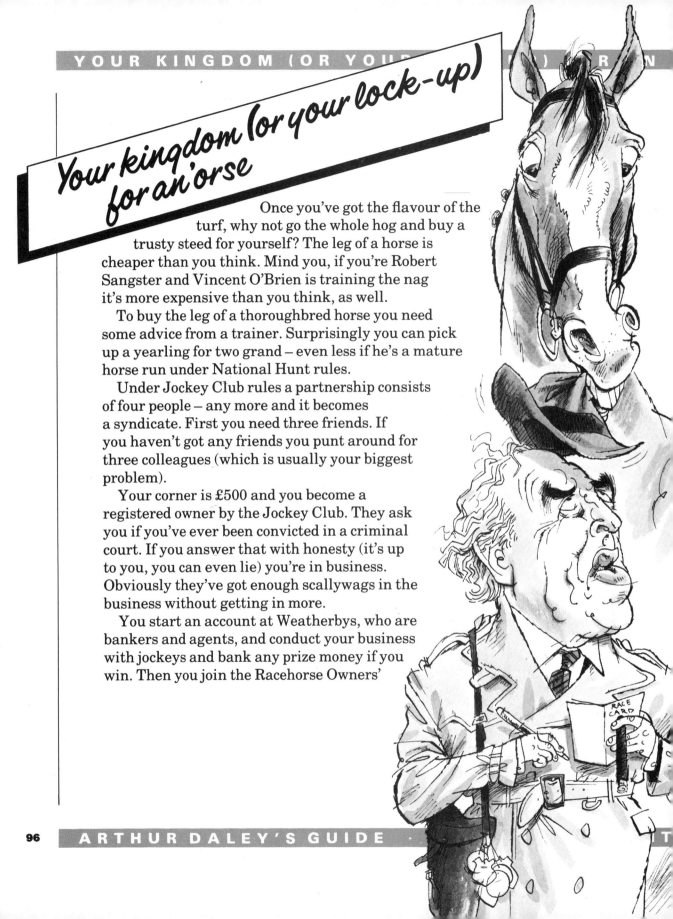

Your kingdom (or your lock-up) for an 'orse

Once you've got the flavour of the turf, why not go the whole hog and buy a trusty steed for yourself? The leg of a horse is cheaper than you think. Mind you, if you're Robert Sangster and Vincent O'Brien is training the nag it's more expensive than you think, as well.

To buy the leg of a thoroughbred horse you need some advice from a trainer. Surprisingly you can pick up a yearling for two grand – even less if he's a mature horse run under National Hunt rules.

Under Jockey Club rules a partnership consists of four people – any more and it becomes a syndicate. First you need three friends. If you haven't got any friends you punt around for three colleagues (which is usually your biggest problem).

Your corner is £500 and you become a registered owner by the Jockey Club. They ask you if you've ever been convicted in a criminal court. If you answer that with honesty (it's up to you, you can even lie) you're in business. Obviously they've got enough scallywags in the business without getting in more.

You start an account at Weatherbys, who are bankers and agents, and conduct your business with jockeys and bank any prize money if you win. Then you join the Racehorse Owners'

Association and they'll give you a sticker for your motor windscreen for the important meetings.

The trainer wants about £80 a week (your corner is £20) plus vet fees, transport and a box of cube sugar for Hi Ho Silver.

For your modest outlay it's going to knock you back at least £40 a week. The jockey likes a drink and the stable boy ditto. Should the nag win the trainer takes his cut, and you're supposed to give him a present. He's always happy to accept a new pair of green wellies and a Royal Doulton coffee service.

Think of it this way, what can you get for £40 a week?

1 a Chinese meal for two
2 rent of a bedsitter in Battersea
3 a good shirt
4 forty pints of Tennants lager
5 four parking fines
6 a single fare from Euston to Glasgow Central (and you'll still have a couple of bob for a cheese roll and a plastic glass of lager).

What's in it for you? Well, the pleasure of driving to Doncaster on a rainy day and seeing your horse beaten out of sight by an expensive horse, but meeting stone rich owners (the country set chatting about fat stock prices and how they had to shoot a fox recently). You'll meet iffy bookmakers too and shake the hand of Willy Carson.

What you're really getting is respect. With a carpark sticker on the windscreen you can park outside Fortnum & Mason's. The local newspaper will report your activities like 'Well-known local businessman and racehorse-owner appeared at the Crown Court accused of . . .' You can show a photograph of your horse to cronies and bend their ears how you met the Aly Khan, John Banks, Brough Scott and Jenny Pitman.

This horse is money in the bank, a collateral of your honesty, an indication that you are a pillar of society. If you can walk with racehorse owners (and the Queen has got a few horses) you're looking at the stars. Mind you, after three years when you haven't got a penny piece out of it and you don't need any more respect, then you sell him to another owner or even to the dogmeat factory.

I mean, we're all horse lovers but we're not daft as well.

The sport of kings

The true Englishman loves the horse. From the Royal Family to the lowest gas-meter thief there is a bond between every true Brit – they like the gee-gees.

There is a difference between going to Hackney dogs and Goodwood, just as there is between dropping into Paul Raymond's Revuebar and the Royal Ballet. The people are different. You might meet the Queen at Ascot but you'll never see her at Leyton Orient.

But alas, as in many fields of endeavour the sacred turf is occasionally besmirched by villainy. And as it happens you may as well make your racing pay. I've said it a hundred times and I'll repeat again: there is no such thing as a racing certainty . . . unless. . . ?

I despise mug punters, the kind of people who bet on every race. The only bloke who wins on every race is Joe Coral. Moderation is the name of the game. You need information, which means a large circle of iffy trainers, jockeys and stable boys.

Sometimes I think that the horses are a bit iffy as well. As in all species there are criminals – man-eating tigers, neurotic dogs, wild cats, mad cows – so why not villainous racehorses? They're highly strung as you would imagine, being thoroughbreds – they can be contrary, a bit lippy. Some of them see the winning post ahead and they decide not to try. This is one of the many problems of picking out a genuine steed when he's going to carry your dough.

When you see a horse with a line of doughnuts before him and he beats some well-fancied runners, you know there's a bit of villainy around. The fact is with a modicum of intelligence and the Timeform black book you should be able to pick a winner. You're going to say 'How come the newspapers don't get them?' Well, they do sometimes. In any race of between six to twelve runners there are only three horses with a decent chance. The rest are just making up the numbers.

The reason why Captain Cohen (or whatever his name is) doesn't get more winners is because he has to pick *one*, not *three*. Your real astute punter won't bet more than a dozen times a season. For a start he rigs the odds.

What we're looking for is a small meeting on a Bank Holiday with a race with six runners and a cast-iron favourite. On a holiday Monday there may be fourteen meetings and some of the courses have bad communication with the major bookmakers' offices. Occasionally the course bookmakers have to use public telephone boxes.

The odds reflect the market. Let us assume that the bookies offer a price on a well fancied runner, say 5 to 4. At the course, money talks. With a couple of grand you can change the pattern of the odds. That kind of money on the third favourite would make him a 'false' favourite and the real favourite would drift in the odds. Within minutes he could be 7 to 2. A few judicious bets on the other runners and our well fancied 'favourite' is going to be an outsider.

Back at the ranch, in dear old London, dozens of £5, £10 and £20 bets have been placed in your local betting shop. If you don't get too greedy you've got a result. Try for half a million and the bookmakers will block the winnings and cry conspiracy; if you go for £150,000 they pay up as sweet as a nut. They know they've been done but the aggravation of investigating the coup and the bad publicity will be almost as expensive as paying up. And just remember, there's no such thing as a racing certainty. Many betting coups are scuppered by a villainous horse who doesn't know he's supposed to win. I mean, they're not all that clever, are they? If they were they'd be book-makers instead of shlepping around a racecourse.

ALTERNATIVE BOOKMAKERS

You won't find their names in *Time Out*; you have to know somebody who knows somebody.

That somebody is against the punitive betting tax which nicks ten per cent from the stake or the winnings. Why pay tax indeed? There are certain bookmakers who won't deduct tax, the kind of bookmak-ers who don't pay their dues to the Inland Revenue or Customs and Excise. They're usually called Commission Agents and they get three per cent on every bet they place with one of the independent large bookmakers. Eventually it goes to the likes of William Hill or Ladbrokes anyway. It's good business for everybody, particularly as most big punters lose like everybody else. But at least they've got the satisfaction of beating the system, so they think.

Don't ask a commission agent to take your 10p ITV Seven flutter. He's not in that business; he's only interested in big wagers. And a note of caution: if you've got an account with Ladbrokes and you can't pay you'll get a polite letter saying that you've overlooked their account and a week later you'll get another letter and maybe one from the legal department as well. Your friendly commission agent doesn't have the secretarial skills. It's more likely a knock on the door *not* at three o'clock in the morning but at any time.

Antiques don't have to be old

Every man is his own Arthur Negus these days. The most humble junk-shop owner wants an arm and a leg for a bakelite table lamp (Co-op, circa 1948) because it's old – well, it's not all that old, is it?

One of the problems of antiques is that you don't know where they've been. Nevertheless, one of the basic accoutrements of the gentleman's chambers or gaff is an Adam fireplace. Robert Adam was the guv'nor, the Tom Finney of the fireplace game: his simple design was the Cortina of the mantelpiece business.

He was knocking them out in his factory like a good 'un. Within a few years everybody was at it. And they're still at it.

An original Adam fireplace (authenticated) will cost about £7,000. A copy made in 1790 would be about £1,000 and a modern copy would cost you £500.

It's up to you.

Street of ink

I've never trusted the newspapers since my little bit of bother at the Crown Court. I have to confess that some of the motors had been tampered with – but that was largely because these cars were so superbly maintained that the prospective customers wouldn't believe the mileage on the clock. Stand on me, these motors were magnificent. In market terms they were a steal. That was another problem: I didn't know they were on the missing list – if I may use a common euphemism.

I have to agree with my brief (and if you want to talk about a 'steal' what about *his* fee?) that my punctiliousness was amiss in that period. There were three iffy characters in the dock with me – main chancers who I hardly knew – and my brief actually used the immortal words of Brian London, the Blackpool Rock – 'I'm a prawn in the game.' As you can imagine, the local newspapers gave me blanket coverage. 'Er indoors could hardly walk down the street without peeping toms asking her views on life, road tax, the traffic problem and penal reform.

I am well known in the Street of Ink and Shame. I have drunk with them in their squalid taverns, where they spend their time composing their expenses sheets, fumbling in the pockets of their ill-formed suits, producing pieces of silver on the counter, nudging you and saying, 'I'll have a large one, old boy.' They're a bad lot. However, a man has to read what they write if only to find out what happened at Craven Cottage last night. Reading newspapers is not a gentleman's pursuit. All I can offer are a few pointers to show the reasonable and the diabolical.

You won't go too far by taking the following:

Daily Telegraph	they share many of my views and the crossword is always good for a laugh.
Daily Mail	it won't damage your brain. Most Sierra drivers read this one.
Country Life	for those who remember England as it used to be, and it's handy if you're going to thatch your sixth-floor flat.
Motor	very important just in case there's a new Korean motor on the market.
Field	a key publication for people who want to shoot things.
Boxing News	it's getting a bit bolshie these days, using words like 'establishment' and 'awesome' – that means anybody who's got a decent left hook – but it's still a good read.

Now we go to the enemy within, reading material I don't want to see in my home.

The Mirror	a red rag, a *Pravda* with tits and bums. It almost supported the miners.
The Guardian	all those caring journalists, and the women are the worst. it's not *real* writing.
New Musical Express Tatler and Marxism Today	from the same stable; they're both trying to destroy the class system.
Time Out	not as revolutionary as the two above but they're trying. And what with their films and plays you don't know where you are.

Wisdom and the cabbie

Know your enemy. A lippy taxi-driver (known as a cabbie) is one of the most dangerous urban species known to us.

Ever since that little know-it-all won *Mastermind* a couple of years ago they all think they're the font of universal wisdom. 'You been to Florida, guv? I always go there for my holidays. I tell you what . . . we're fifteen years behind them. It's a different country, innit?' Would you call that wisdom?

The thing is, they feel equal to the customers. Just because they're self-employed it doesn't mean they're *not* workers. And even if you know all the one-way streets in the West End (which they don't usually anyway) that doesn't mean they can solve all the economic problems of the Western world. A lot of the time they're doing you a favour. 'D'you know who I had in the back of the cab yesterday? . . . Jimmy Greaves/Bob Monkhouse/Jimmy Savile/ Petula Clark/Henry Kissinger/the whole West Indies cricket team/ Denis Thatcher or Lulu's brother-in-law.'

'Fascinating,' you say as you're trying to read a letter from your accountant.

'Interesting bloke,' says the cabbie. 'No side . . . just like us.' (That's presumptuous . . . 'just like us' . . . as if you were equals. That's why I started a mini-cab company.)

Mini-cab drivers don't know where they're going but at least they're quieter. You ask one to take you to Haymarket or Park Lane and he's thumbing through his *Reader's Digest Atlas of the World* as if it's in the back streets of Rio de Janeiro.

Mini-cab drivers do it all by guesswork. 'Three fifty,' they announce as they glance at their imaginary milometer after they've taken you at least half a mile out of the way. But they're grateful if you give them a tip. Your real cabbie expects it by right. You give him twenty pence for a £3-fare and he'll give it back to you with a smirk saying: 'You keep it, pal. Your need is greater than mine.'

If a cabbie loses his licence the chances are that he'll become a builder or a plumber.

Art for art and gawd's sake

Don't leave art to the experts. Art belongs to the people – the people with the dough.

If you think that builders are dubious characters who know nothing about their particular trade, then clock at an art gallery. If you're trying to sell an old painting (I get hold of them occasionally) it's like selling an old motor. 'Has it been in your family long? Did you spill semolina on it? How many owners? And it has no intrinsic value, you know.' Within two minutes you realise that he knows as much about it as you. You're back into Warren Street.

Old Tom Keating, the master faker, blew the gaffe on the gallery scam: he was knocking out half a dozen Old Masters during a weekend. If you can get hold of a Keating, buy it – they're valuable now. You see, everything's got its price.

Modern art is a different game. Some of these painters get awards from the Arts Council, which is a bit like getting an up-market Giro cheque. They'll have a go at anything – bits of plywood, hardboard, nothing like canvas. They'll use acrylic paint, emulsion, satin sheen, bits of broken plates or whatever.

The funny thing is some of them are earning well. Look at that David Hockney with his swimming pools or that Patrick Caulfield (chairs are his thing – painting them, not making them) or Lucien Freud (painting his relatives as if they're having a hard time) and that Francis Bacon (doing things like you might find in a halal butcher's window).

What you won't find in these pictures are sunsets, horses, trees or even dogs. And how do you know that they're good? If you're buying a reproduction – you can get them on simulated canvas, you know – you're getting something decent, tested by time, and not forever explaining what it means to your guests.

'There you go, Tel –
that's modern art for you.'

Fly with me

For a thrusting entrepreneur like myself the annual holiday is not important. Two days in Brighton is good enough for me. But I realise that our weaker brethren have to get away occasionally. As well as having a rest there is also the problem of lying low or avoiding being interviewed by busybodies, whether they be Inland Revenue inspectors, Customs and Excise or Old Bill.

The chaps like exotic places, as far away from London as possible. They like to think of themselves as trail-blazers – before all the Germans get there. Brazil is an obvious place – plenty of currant bun, beautiful beaches, handsome ladies and as a bonus you can say hello to old Biggsie.

Marbella is almost part of London now. There you can meet old friends, stay at their villas, plot schemes, have a chat with your bank manager or discuss your current case with the officer in charge. The rest of Europe is unimportant. Majorca was handy in the Fifties. Ibiza had its time in the Sixties and San Tropez got the elbow when the ordinary civilians pitched their tents around it.

Members of the alternative society want to impress the neighbours and their peers. The top spots are now:

1 Mexico (particularly Acapulco)
2 Hawaii
3 Brazil (at carnival time)
4 Barbados (at any time)
5 Florida

You will never meet the chaps in Leningrad, Albania, the Greek Islands, Madeira, Warsaw, Germany or India.

You can just get by if you've been to Singapore, Morocco, the Seychelles, South Africa, Madagascar or even Bermuda.

A real gentleman doesn't even go abroad. He might just go to Brighton, Eastbourne, Scarborough or the Isle of Wight but more likely to Scotland to shoot some smoked salmon.

Old Dave of the Winchester Club decided to take a cruise to Gibraltar last year, and got very excited about it before he went. Obviously I helped him out with his leisure wear and a pair of water-skis, just in case he got a tow. Unfortunately I didn't have a dinner jacket in stock. He said he thought he might be invited to the captain's table, but I told him: 'You've paid good money for your ticket so you don't want to eat with the staff, do you?' They do all kinds of strokes, don't they?

Banks are for people

If you want to start an account with a false name (is there any other kind?) always see the manager, not a clerk. Don't take any lip either. Remember, it's your money, not theirs. The bank manager is working for you, not vice versa. So, make sure he's aware of this.

He may ask for references. You say – quietly and firmly – that you prefer your financial affairs to be confidential. In a more urgent tone, you say: 'Don't you realise, my good man, that I'm giving you *money*? If anything, I should be the one demanding references. I'm trusting you. You hear terrible things about iffy bank managers . . .'

All I can say is that I've never been refused.

If you draw money from a bank where you have no account you are called a bank robber. Some people have cheque cards, others have sawn-off shotguns.

Meeting your maker or you versus the inland revenue

They're after you. They actually believe that the money is theirs. This is still a free country but they're trying to make it into a Gulag Archipelago. I used to be idealistic – that's when I was a Socialist and I thought everybody should have an Austin 7. Then I realised that they believe in taxes. Now I think only good people get Jaguars and Rollers – those who deserve them.

When you hear that the Inspector from Inland Revenue wants to see you, don't flinch. They're only human. You must be strong and fearless. It's you against them, it's the Alamo, St Crispin's Day, Fulham against Liverpool away. It's Greek meets Greek. (I use a literary metaphor; to be honest, I've never met a bubble in the Inland Revenue. They're too busy grilling up their kebabs, ladling out the taramasalata and sending postal orders over to the old folks back home.)

To meet the Inspector you have to dress in a particular way. You're going to plead poverty so you don't want to appear with a spanking-new Crombie, do you? My advice is:

1 A Marks and Spencer (or C & A) suit which is at least five years old. A shirt with a slightly frayed collar. Terylene tie.

2 No accoutrements of the good life, e.g. no flash wristwatch, no Parker, Mont Blanc or Sheaffer pen. If you've got to have a pen try a plastic Bic. No cufflinks – a dead giveaway for a gentleman. No cigars. A Wills Whiff maybe and even a Panatella. If you produce a dented Old Holborn tin, all the better.

Don't go too strong otherwise they'll think you're a penny stamp or an eccentric millionaire.

You'll be surprised how much information they know about you. Well, deny everything. Your demeanour is one of frankness, naïvety and self-pity, a pawn in the awful game of low finance, an honest man who doesn't understand the machinations of our contemporary life today.

They'll ask you about your company. Right away you're on the offensive. 'It's not a real company,' you say. 'It's just a name, not an

active company. It's a sentimental thing – a mere memory of my youth when I had ambition and a dream of being a captain of industry and commerce . . . like Robert Maxwell. He's done well, hasn't he? But these days I'm more-or-less semi-retired.'

You've got to be ready for the next question. The Inspector is worried about his mortgage and whether he can ditch his Sinclair computer and buy a Sinclair electric scooter instead? If you have to make these kinds of decisions you're not going to have a lot of sympathy with your average Jaguar-owner.

'Company car,' he mutters.

'That's not mine,' you say. 'You've got it all wrong. That's my uncle's. I said to him, "Cedric, why do you need a car like that . . . you being an old age pensioner?" And he said it was an old man's folly. He never uses it. And you know what, he said, "You use it, Arthur . . . you not having wheels of your own." Wasn't that nice, eh?'

Obviously, you've done your homework, haven't you? You have to have an uncle called Cedric and your motor is, in fact, registered in his name. (For that he gets a bottle of Drambuie every Christmas. You've got to take care of your own, haven't you?)

The Inspector is still thinking about his Sinclair. I'm worried about North Sea oil, he's fretting about power cuts. And he wants to know if I use the motor for work or business.

'Ah, work,' you say nostalgically. 'Even the school-leavers can't get a job. What chance of me getting one, a man of my age? They don't want mature, experienced old soldiers like me. These days I help people who can't help themselves. That's the only job I do.'

Is the Inspector impressed? Probably not, but what can he do about it? You should press on:

'A lot of the time,' you say, 'I use the motor to take old people down the Darby and Joan club or if they want to go to hospital. Or at election time. No favours. If they want to vote – even for some looney – I'll take them down to the polling station.'

Now he's going to pry into your personal life. He's confused because you have no assets and no regular income.

'How do you get by then,' he says (and he's genuinely interested), 'what with food, clothes, the Duke of Kent and the occasional sherbet?'

'I often ask that meself,' you say. 'It's all down to 'er indoors. She does manage well. . . .'

'Hang about, Arthur,' he says (obviously we're on Christian-name terms by now) 'she's got a little Metro, two kids at a private school—'

'I don't know how she does it,' you say. 'Incredible woman. Just between you and me, I think she's got a few pennies in the Post Office.'

And then right out of the blue he says, 'What d'you reckon about that Sinclair runabout?'

'I tell you what,' you say, 'wouldn't you fancy a little Renault instead? I might be able to help you there. . . .'

English as it's spoke and writ

Sometimes it's difficult to understand accounts in the newspapers or the argot of the streets.

There are things called euphoniums* – different ways of saying crude words or expressions. For example:

model = brass
Mayfair hostess = brothel-keeper
West End businessman = gangster
a well known sportsman = owes money to several
    gambling clubs
security consultant = minder, or even hit-man
clip on the ear or clout = G.B.H.
had it away = a successful robbery

Thus, if a West End businessman (gangster) is talking about a colleague and 'he's due for spanking', he really means he should be shot, bayoneted and garrotted, and that's just for starters.

---

* *Editor's note:* euphemisms

A useful lexicon

There are many pitfalls for the beginner.

You use these words in a natural way. Beware of overkill or you'll sound like a right walley.

There are certain rules: usually you abbreviate rhyming slang expressions (e.g. minces = eyes, *never* mince pies, which is the root). But all rules can be broken. Thus, you will say 'tea leaf' for thief, never 'tea' – it doesn't scan.

Be wary of out-dated slang like 'lolly' for money, which went out with Stanley Matthews and long shorts. Don't be gauche. On my landlord's life, I have never heard somebody say 'pig's ear' for beer, or 'round the houses' for trousers. Anyway, who wants to have beer if you can have a large vodka and slimline instead? And if you have to refer to trousers (who would want to in mixed company anyway?) you can always use 'strides'.

Say it this way	Root	Word
Aris	Aristotle = bottle and glass = arse	bum or bottom
		gravy
Army & Navy		locked in a cell (prisoner)
banged up		
	Barnet Fair	hair
barnet		pocket
bin (or sky = sky rocket)		
	birdlime	time (as in prison)
bird		one who steals a girl from another man
bird-bandit		to rob a payroll or money delivery (usually outside on the street)
blag		
	boatrace	face
		dope
boat		skint
Bob Hope	boracic lint	no courage or nerve
boracic	see Aris	prostitute
bottle-out	brass nail	Greek
brass	bubble and squeak	talk
bubble	rabbit and pork	look
bunny	butcher's hook	three months in prison
butchers		squatter
carpet		ten
Chelsea potter	cock and hen	stranger
cockle	Connaught Rangers (an old regiment)	
Connaught		sun
		fingerprints
currant bun		jacket
dabs	Desmond Hackett (well known sporting journalist in the '40s and '50s)	
Desmond		
		turning Queen's evidence
doing a Royal		certainty
dot on the card	a nap selection	house or flat
drum or gaff		

Say it this way	Root	Word
dubbed up		placed in a cell (e.g. 'I was dubbed up with John Whatsisname')
Duke of Kent		bent or rent
face		a well known criminal or a celebrity
farmers (or Chalfont St Giles)	Farmer Giles	piles
fit-up		false evidence
firm		a gang
gas meter thieves		minor thieves (always derisory – an unimportant criminal)
Germans	German bands	hands
gee-up		encourage someone (a verbal prod)
gold watch	scotch	scotch whisky
grass	snake in the grass	the lowest of the low – betraying colleagues
Hampsteads	Hampstead Heath	teeth
in the frame		the prime suspect
ice cream	ice cream freezer	geezer
iron	iron hoof	poof
Jacks	Jacks Alive	five (fiver)
Jack the Ripper		kipper or stripper
jam	jamjar	car
jug		bank
K or a long 'un		a thousand
Kosher	(from the computer world) (Hebrew) according to Jewish food laws	the genuine thing, true
lemon	lemon dash	flash
loop-the-loop		soup
luke	Lucozade	spade (black person)
make one		a prison escape or planned robbery
marking your card		advice
a meet		an appointment or date

Say it this way	Root	Word
minces	mince pies	eyes
monkey		£500
moody		wrong
mutton	Mutt & Jeff	deaf
a nonce	nonsense	child-sex offenders
nosh		food
Oliver	Oliver Twist	pissed, drunk
on your Jack	Jack Jones	alone
Peckham	Peckham Rye	tie
penny stamp		tramp
peter		safe or cell
pony		£25
porkies	pork pies	lies
Quaker	Quaker Oat	coat
Richard	Richard the Third	bird (girl)
rickit		a mistake
rock 'n' roll		dole
Roller		a Rolls-Royce
Ruby	Ruby Murray	curry
the S.P.	starting prices	genuine information
scarper	Scapa Flow	go
score		twenty
Sexton	Sexton Blake	steak or fake
shmutter	(Yiddish)	clothes or suit
shooter		revolver
shtum	(Yiddish)	be quiet
shtuk	(Yiddish)	misfortune, trouble
snout		police informer or tobacco
spiel	(Yiddish)	patter/gambling
stand-at-ease		cheese
steam tugs		drugs
the strength		real information
stretch		a twelve-month prison sentence (but you could say 'I done a four stretch')
		find out
		wig
suss it out		
a syrup (occasionally Irish)	syrup of figs or Irish jig	thief
tea leaf		Chinese
tiddlywink	chink	alone
Tod	Tod Sloane	jewellery
Tom	tomfoolery	

Say it this way	Root	Word
tweedle *or* on the tweedle		to substitute a fake article for a genuine item. Used in jewellery shops. With sleight of hand the 'tweedler' steals an expensive ring and leaves a worthless but similar ring in its place
weekend gangsters		people who go to work but mix with criminals in the evening
weighed in	(bookmakers pay out winnings only after the jockeys have been weighed in)	a debt paid
weighed off		the sentence after the defendant has been found guilty
wind-up		a verbal trick/joking/teasing

Special note
Old Bill, the filth, the pigs, the dirt, the law, Mr Plod, the fuzz, coppers, rozzers, cozzers, bogeys, woodentops (uniformed officers), the splits (plain clothes officers – archaic) and many other expressions – police

There is, of course, lots of confusion. Ordinary working-class Londoners might use the word 'bird' for a girl. Those in the twilight zone, denizens of the demi-monde as I like to call it, would more likely use 'bird' for time in prison. For example, 'He did plenty of bird,' etc.

This is a living language. Vogue names will creep into the vocabulary, e.g. Russell Harty = party (usurping the more traditional Moriarty. I still use that myself). Sentiment is also involved. If you've always used the Donalds (Donald Peers* = ears), it's difficult to change. There is a certain poetry in the expression: 'He gave me the G.B.H. of the Donalds' instead of 'bending my ear'.

---

* Donald Peers, popular singer in the '40s and '50s.

The last journey

It happens to us all – there is a happy release and we go to a better place where there are no Inland Revenue people and we don't need MoTs.

We've grafted all our lives, there's a bit of the folding green under the floorboards, you've put your feet up and are holding a last large vodka and slimline in your fist and then – whammo, the grim reaper calls your number, the last invoice that nobody can duck out from; it's the final demand, and they ain't kidding.

If you have paid your dues you're entitled to have a decent funeral. Members of the alternative society like a good funeral. The theory is that you came into this world without a fanfare so you may as well go out with a bang. That means, at least, an oak coffin with gilt handles, ten hired limousines and a Russell Harty that goes on till the early hours. Wreaths are requested, indeed *demanded*, and the floral tributes should be as large, ornate and gaudy as you can afford – intricate arrangements with messages like: 'One of the Best' or 'Goodbye Charlie – one of our own'. And there should be as many enemies as friends among the congregation. Incidentally, the people I'm talking about want to be buried, not cremated.

Villains are sentimental people. They like to shed a tear. 'At least he never grassed,' they would say about a feared rival. 'Let's give him a good farewell – just in case he comes back.'

The party is important. Plenty of booze ('Charlie always liked a good drink') and the catering should be left to the womenfolk or to one of the chaps who knows about it. For a rough guide I would suggest:

200 individual meat pies
1 gallon of taramasalata
1 family size jar of Branston pickle
1 gallon of coleslaw
1 gallon of potato salad
1 Stilton
24 French loaves

Apart from the ordinary alcoholic drinks remember that there will also be ladies at the function. Stock up on sweet sherry, snowballs, egg flip, pina colada, Babycham, banana daiquiri and German wine such as Liebfraumilch.

You will hear lots of pearls of philosophy from the mourners, such as: 'In life we are all on remand, in a sense, until the day of judgement when the great beak up in the sky weighs us off . . .

Where he's going it's a bit like an open prison – plenty of gardening, a healthy life and nothing to worry about.'

If the deceased was a business colleague you may have a problem. The bereaved have a cavalier attitude to commerce and it may be a long time before the estate is settled. What happens if the deceased owed you some dough? Obviously, you can't knock on the door when the family are prising up the floorboards. I suggest a civil and sensitive letter. For example:

Dear Doreen,

As you know, Charlie was one of my greatest friends. We had a special relationship right from the time when he had that little bit of bother at the Bailey and I was surety for his bail (twenty grand, as I remember it, and I was deeply relieved when he appeared at the trial, and what an incredible result it was!)

I am sure that Charlie would be happy to see that his old pals will be taken care of. I know he was very ill; but did he say anything about my two grand? We were doing a little bit of business – South Korean videos, one of which I noticed in your sitting room during the tasteful party. As in life, Charlie settled up promptly and now that he has gone to a better place (not suggesting that there's anything wrong with your own delightful maisonette) I'm sure he'd like you to dip into your purse and finalise the transaction.

Incidentally, nice to see your son back in the manor.

My deepest condolences,

As ever

Arthur Daley

PS: I was going to remind Charlie when I saw him in the hospital but he had a lot on his mind at the time.
My deepest sympathy.

I may say, I never even got a sausage from the cow.